C000135890

Malcolm Walton was born in 1950. He qualified as a solicitor in 1973 and practised law briefly before entering a career of property management and investment in 1973. Over the last 20 years he has gained considerable experience in property investment and development, initially as a principal and in later years acting on behalf of clients. He is now Executive Chairman of Senate International, a company advising both UK and overseas residents on buying residential property to let.

Malcolm Walton is married with five children and lives on a farm in Hertfordshire.

PROPERTY
INVESTOR

*How to Profit
from Buying Residential Property to Let*

Malcolm Walton

A CAMBRIDGE TITLES PUBLICATION

Published 1998 by

Cambridge Titles Limited
The Square House
Church Street
Little Shelford
Cambridge CB2 5HG
UK

Tel: 01223 847383
Fax: 01223 847799

British Library Cataloguing in Publication Data
A catalogue record for this book is available
from the British Library.

ISBN 0 9531057 0 9

Printed in the UK by Biddles Limited.

PREFACE

I decided in April 1997 to write a book about buying property for investment purposes and it took nearly nine months from start to finish. Writing a book is an interesting experience, not least because when writing on a specialist subject, such as in *Property Investor*, it forces a major concentration of the mind and, in my case, to some extent the writer re-learns lessons learnt many years ago.

Investment in and development of property have a strong appeal to many people – far greater than probably any other form of investment. I think the reasons for this are that firstly, property is one of the basic material necessities of life and secondly, many people harbour a desire, often unspoken, of being a successful investor or dealer in property.

As far as I am aware, *Property Investor* is the first book to be published in the United Kingdom that gives those outside the property profession a thorough insight and guide as to how to successfully invest in and develop residential property. I believe my book is successful in achieving this. However, the real test is how valuable this book would be to me if I was investing in property today with little or no previous experience. I believe, under those circumstances, it would be of immense help and, if I am right, my ambitions for the book have been achieved.

I would like to thank the following without whose help I could not have achieved the writing and completion of the book. Firstly, I would like to acknowledge the special part played by Lynne Norris, who steadfastly and bravely worked countless hours in typing and retyping endless drafts and amendments. Special thanks go to Bridget Warrington and Jo Davidson who provided the technical and professional assistance to turn my initial drafts into a readable and professional work. Finally, my special thanks and love go to my wife, Hennie, who gave me much needed support and encouragement, and who told me that she had always wanted to be married to a writer!

Malcolm Walton

CONTENTS

LIST OF EXAMPLES

INTRODUCTION

The purpose of writing *Property Investor* is to provide a highly practical guide to investing in residential property. Its aim is to be equally helpful to either the reader who already owns investment property or to the reader who is proposing to buy residential property for investment purposes for the first time. This is not a technical book padded out with draft leases and recitals of legislation; instead it is a book based on experience. It explains to the potential investor how to identify the best opportunities and maximise returns whether or not a professional adviser is used.

Property Investor gives the reader fundamental guidelines. Property prices constantly move up, down and sideways, as do interest rates, and therefore cannot be accurately forecast. If an investor 'bets on the market' by buying an average property at what he regards to be the bottom of the market, then sells that average property at what he regards to be the top of the market, this may be successful. However, reading the tops and bottoms of the property market is not within the scope of this book. Indeed in an era of low inflation, such a strategy probably has little purpose. Instead, this book explains matters without knowledge of which the investor will be unable to identify the best opportunities (other than by luck) and may well fail to recognise some of the pitfalls of investing in residential property until it is too late.

Successful investment in residential property is, once armed with the right knowledge, a simple, enjoyable and profitable process. When managed correctly, an investment property gives the same satisfaction as owning your own business, which in fact is exactly what it is. Part of you is suddenly self-employed, but there is also a fall-back position in that all or part of your new property business can always be delegated to somebody else.

Over the last few years there has been a huge rise in interest in investing in residential property to let. Of particular significance is the fact that it has been individual investors themselves that have recognised the attractiveness of investment in residential property. This interest is not emerging because of the introduction of tax breaks, or as a result of promotions by professional advisers or even newspapers. It is true that there is now endorsement of the idea by, for example, the Association of Residential Letting Agents (Arla) which has launched its 'Buy to Let' scheme. In addition, some of the property editors of national newspapers are writing about the amount of money now being spent by private individuals on residential property to let, and to a lesser extent commenting on the attractions of the idea.

To give an indication of the number of people now investing in residential property, Arla reported in early 1998 that since launching its 'Buy to Let' scheme, £575 million worth of new property had been brought into the private rental sector.

How do people usually decide what to invest their money in?

1. If they decide to put their money into banks or building societies, they make their own decisions as to which bank or building society to invest in depending on published interest rates being offered.
2. If they decide to put their money in personal equity plans (PEP), unit trusts or pensions/savings plans, then again they usually make the decision as a result of rates published in national newspapers and magazines.
3. If they decide to invest in stocks, shares, gilts or other financial securities, they take advice from stockbrokers or other financial advisers, or they back their own judgement by reading published information about individual stocks and shares.

Who, therefore, is advising all these individuals to invest in residential property? The answer is no one. Primarily they are making the decisions themselves. Stockbrokers and financial advisers are, in reality, highly unlikely to recommend property as an investment for the simple reason that it is not in their interest to do so. Financial advisers make their livings by earning commission on the products that they recommend. So, when a person seeks advice from a financial adviser on what to do with £60,000, it would be an unusual financial adviser who would recommend that the person goes away and looks for a property investment to purchase instead. Even if the financial adviser manages to obtain a fee for arranging the mortgage and possibly shares an acquisition fee with a buying agent who advises on the purchase of the property, the reward to the financial adviser would normally be much less than he would receive from recommending a pension plan, a PEP or stocks and shares.

What about estate agents – don't they recommend the advantages of buying property for investment? Yes they do, but they are not in a position to advise impartially which property to buy. Estate agents act for the seller of the property. They act purely in the interests of the seller and their whole being is geared to generating sales commission. What some estate agents do is suggest which of the properties on their books are suitable for investment purposes. However, other than a handful of specialist estate agents in central London, none even attempt to give a full buying for investment service. Even the ones that do provide such a service usually have a conflict of interest as they are purporting to advise investor purchasers while at the same time doing everything possible to sell the property for the vendor, from whom they obtain their commission, regardless of the actual real merits of the property as an investment.

Some estate agents will, for a fee from the purchaser, agree to identify a suitable property for investment purposes that they have not been instructed to sell. However, except at the top end of the market (over £500,000) the results are rarely satisfactory. Estate agents are not used to time-consuming assessments and inspections of properties that other estate agents are selling, and rarely have the in-house expertise to provide a full package service.

There are now, however, a sprinkling of specialist firms advising purely on investment in residential property. Currently numbering probably less than 20 over the whole of the United Kingdom, these specialists offer a genuine, complete package acquisition service acting only for the investor purchaser. These buying agents, as we will call them, are, with one or two exceptions, still small in size and their existence is unknown to the majority of people who are interested in buying residential property for investment. They do, however, provide a truly specialist service to investors and most of these firms are now expanding rapidly (see Useful Addresses).

One of the major decisions to be made by investors in residential property is whether to use buying agents for the whole investment process, or whether to use them or a letting and management company for only part of the process (for example, letting and management but not other parts such as identifying the property). Even if an investor does decide to use professional advisers throughout the investment process, this book will help to ensure that the right professional advisers are chosen in the first place, and secondly that the best advice is obtained from them. There are currently still so few buying agents that many towns and cities in the United Kingdom are not covered by their services. In those locations the investor has little choice but largely to 'go it alone' other than in respect of mortgage sourcing, and letting and management.

NOTE *Throughout the book 'he' and 'his' are to be interpreted as 'he or she' and 'his or her'.*

CHAPTER 1

Why invest in residential property?

There are various reasons why so many individuals have recently become interested in investing in residential property. However, the obvious one – that the residential property market is currently (1998) rising – is a contributory factor rather than the main reason. What this recent upturn has done is to help kick-start the move to invest in residential property.

A change of direction over the century

Until around the turn of the century, the vast majority (in excess of 90 per cent) of houses were owned by investors who rented them out. Only a very small proportion of the population owned their own houses and the concept of investing in residential property was as well established as investing in stocks, shares or in bank deposits. What changed all this was successive government legislation which gave more and more security to tenants and less and less protection to landlords by way of both rent controls and provisions giving security of tenure. As a result of this legislation, investment by both individuals and institutions reduced dramatically during the course of the twentieth century. So, from the 1930s, it was an investment medium that was almost entirely disregarded and on which virtually no information was available.

The pendulum began to swing the other way with the passing of the Housing Act in 1988, which made dramatic changes in legislation. The most important development was that provided certain procedures were followed, a landlord could, for the first time in many years, charge an open market rent and be sure of getting possession of his property on issuing the necessary notices. However, the impact of this legislation was minimal at the time because, as many readers will recall, it was in the autumn of 1988 that the UK residential property market, after several years of dramatic increases, began to fall.

The '1980s culture' had led many people to believe that house prices could only go one way – up. So the extent of the fall in prices that started in late 1988 took almost everybody by surprise, shattering many people's confidence in the residential property market. Across most of the United Kingdom, prices continued to fall right through to

1994/95 and therefore the last thing on many people's minds, following the passing of the 1988 Housing Act, was the idea of buying residential property as an investment.

During the early 1990s more and more occupiers decided to rent property rather than purchase, as they no longer had the confidence in the property market that they once had. At the same time, however, property prices fell across the country and as a result many people began to realise that high income yields were available from investing in residential property. These yields, often at that time up to 10 per cent to 11 per cent net, became increasingly attractive as interest rates were repeatedly cut to try to bring the country out of recession. People who had money on deposit in banks and building societies were getting lower and lower returns and were looking for alternative places for their money that would give a better return. It was only at this point that the full impact of the changes offered by the 1988 Housing Act were realised and gradually people started to look at the idea of investing in residential property.

The fundamental attraction of property ownership

While the reasons outlined in the section above explain the awakening of interest, there is another simple reason to explain the underlying popularity of investment in the residential sector. People have a basic instinct to wish to own land and property – it gives an individual a feeling of fundamental security. An investor can look at the property and so regards it, rightly, as a tangible asset. Many people feel psychologically wealthier owning a property rather than owning stocks or shares to the same value – they may not like being referred to as a landlord, but they do like owning property. By comparison, when an investor puts his money into shares of a public company he has no control over that company whatsoever. All he can do is sit and watch the share price go up or down, and all he owns is a share certificate – a piece of paper.

No one needs stocks and shares or bank deposit accounts, they simply want them. When a person owns a house or a flat, he owns something that everybody needs, not just wants. Shelter, like food and clothing, is one of the basic necessities of life. If all else fails, he and his family can go and live in it themselves. The investor is in total control of his property. He is able to decide what type of improvements to make to the property and when to make them. He can decide whether to let and manage the property himself or whether to use a professional management company. If he chooses to use a professional management company that then does not perform satisfactorily, he can change the company. So, the opportunity to be both creative and add value to a property is also a major reason for the attraction of investment in property.

Trends into the next century

Investment in residential property is effectively now available to individuals for the first time since the turn of the century. Given the opportunity after such a long period of 'denial', individuals are reverting to a basic instinct of owning a property as an investment in their own name. The residential investment market will, over the next four or five years, become a form of investment as common to individuals as investing in banks, building societies, shares, unit trusts and pension plans. More and more buying agencies will be set up, not as hybrid estate agents, but as specialists providing purchasers with a complete residential property investment package. The letting and management industry will sooner or later become regulated by Parliament with legislation that will necessitate separate client accounts and a requirement to follow professional guidelines in the same way as solicitors, stockbrokers and financial advisers. As the letting and management market becomes more regulated this, in turn, will further fuel interest in investing in the sector.

At the same time, banks and building societies will become as happy to lend on residential property bought for investment purposes as they currently are to lend on residential property bought for occupation. In fact, to a great extent, this trend is already well under way. Current differentials between the amount banks and building societies are prepared to lend for investment and owner-occupier properties and the interest rates charged will, over the next year or two, entirely disappear.

Parliament has recently taken its first tentative step in encouraging institutional investment in the residential property market by the introduction of Housing Investment Trusts (HITs). Further legislation is likely to be introduced over the next two to three years which will increase the attraction of HITs. Subsequent incentives will then, for the first time since the 1930s, mean that pension funds and insurance companies will start to invest in the residential property market as opposed to confining all their property investments, as they do now, to the commercial property market.

Current legislation permits self-administered pension funds to invest in commercial property only, but it is probable that, within certain limits, legislation will be changed so that residential property will also be permitted. In today's climate, such investment in houses and flats – rather than offices and shops – is more politically correct and will considerably ease the burden on the UK Government to provide dwellings to rent for lower income groups.

All these changes will encourage wider press coverage of investment in residential property and therefore promote more understanding and knowledge of the market. National and local newspapers and specialist magazines will start to carry more information on the residential investment market, and buying agents will produce more performance figures.

When is the right time to invest in property?

Most people agree that the United Kingdom has entered a period of low inflation which is likely to be sustained for many years. Attitudes have changed since the recession of the 1980s and, for the foreseeable future, it is unlikely that we are going to see anything other than an economy producing a relatively stable or gently rising residential property market. These conditions are ideal to breed and nurture the growth of the residential investment market.

A common question asked of many professionals involved in the property business is: what is the property market doing at the moment? While average figures are regularly compiled by the Land Registry and by the big banks and building societies, these figures are in fact meaningless other than to give a general guide to the overall state of the residential market.

The property market in the United Kingdom has always been localised, but never more so than today. If you take the following cities and towns – picked virtually at random – you will find that at any one time each has a property market that is performing differently in one way or another and, in some cases, radically differently: Birmingham, Brighton, Cambridge, Cardiff, Durham, Edinburgh, Glasgow, Great Yarmouth, Hull, London, Manchester, Nottingham, Oxford and Taunton. Each of these cities and towns has, at any one time, different property markets – some rising exceptionally fast, some rising gently, some static and some actually falling.

Each market will itself vary according to the property type: three-bedroom Victorian houses might have gone up in Cambridge by 12 per cent during a 12-month period, while studio flats in Cambridge might only have gone up by 0.5 per cent during the same period. In addition, the bigger cities have their own local markets. For example, London has a multitude of markets such as Battersea, Bayswater, Chelsea, Docklands, Fulham, Hammersmith, Knightsbridge and Pimlico. Each of these local markets has the same variables as a small city such as Cambridge. Each district of the larger city and each smaller town has areas that are more popular, regardless of the property type.

All of this may seem daunting to the private individual investor, but it needn't be. It is these very variables that provide the opportunity to choose an individual property that will outperform the general market. Just as few people successfully invest in the stock market at random but instead identify an individual share, so one of the big attractions of direct investment in residential property is that the investor always has a wide choice from which to identify an individual property that will outperform the market as a whole. The sheer scale of the residential market – the total value of UK housing is in the region of £1,200 billion – means that there is always a selection of outstanding opportunities available.

As the property investment market becomes more established, investors will have the opportunity to invest in funds and unit trusts that will specialise in investing in residential property. These will be promoted as spreading the risk of investors while avoiding the hassles and pitfalls of investing directly in an individual property. No doubt such funds and unit trusts will attract considerable sums of money, but they will never begin to compare with the performance available from buying an individual property in the right location with the right potential for adding value. Nor will they satisfy the basic instinct and security that comes from direct ownership of a whole property, rather than a share of a property.

Normally when people ask what the property market is doing, they are enquiring because they are thinking of selling their own house or perhaps buying a house for occupation. The question is irrelevant to the serious individual property investor because, whether the overall market is rising or falling, there are always individual opportunities where substantial investment returns in the form of capital and income are obtainable. This income is secured by the fact that the current trend of occupiers renting property as an alternative to owning property is likely to continue to grow. Job security is largely a thing of the past and the working population is becoming increasingly mobile. Added to this is the fact that there is no longer any stigma attached to living in a rented house.

Renting your own home while investing in property elsewhere

One trend that is just beginning to emerge is renting the house in which you live while owning one or two properties purely for investment. This configuration offers a financial advantage and is particularly attractive if the house you occupy is in a rural location where rentals in relation to capital values are low.

Suppose an individual has £100,000 in cash. He could buy a property in a rural location with the £100,000 or, alternatively, he could rent a property to the same value where he would pay a rental of no more than around 5 per cent of the capital value – ie £5,000 per annum. With the £100,000 'saved' he could buy a quality investment property in a city likely to show good capital and rental growth. Even if the capital growth of the town property is only the same as the capital growth which he would have enjoyed if he had bought the rural property, assuming an 8.5 per cent net income yield on the investment property he would receive an income of £8,500 a year. This would make him £3,500 a year better off in income terms than if he had bought, rather than rented, the property in the rural location. In addition, structural repairs to the rural property (for example, replacing the roof) would be the responsibility of the landlord and if a period or older country property is rented, the savings would be substantial. The attractions are considerably more marked if more than one investment property is bought by borrowing (see Chapter 4).

How to assess the state of the property market

So what are the actual returns available from investing in residential property? One influencing factor is, of course, what property prices and rental values are doing generally. These are affected by factors beyond an investor's control, namely the state of the economy and government policy.

One thing is fairly certain, however, and that is that house prices are ultimately determined firstly by average earnings and secondly by supply in relation to demand. As can be seen by from the graph below, despite the increase in house prices in some parts of the United Kingdom during 1995–97, house prices still lagged substantially behind average earnings. As regards supply and demand, in 1997 the government estimated that no less than 4.4 million new houses would be needed in the United Kingdom by the year 2016. The amount of land needed for this amount of development is the equivalent of 10 cities the size of Bristol. In theory all these houses will be built, but in practice there will be huge opposition to building on greenfield sites. If the new houses have to be

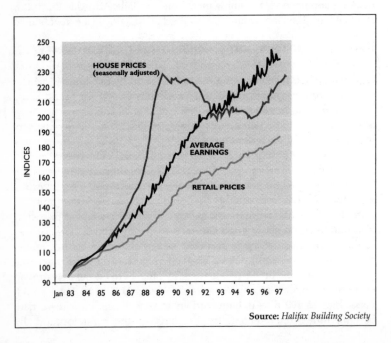

Source: *Halifax Building Society*

accommodated mainly on reclaimed land – so-called 'brownfield sites' – in order to satisfy public opinion, then it is extremely unlikely that the required number of houses will be built within the projected time-scale.

What all this means is that there are underlying, fundamentally sound financial reasons to believe that residential property prices over the next 10 to 20 years will continue to outperform the average inflation rate, quite possibly by a substantial margin.

Making the right decisions

Apart from the general state of the market, there are four main factors that affect the return on investment in residential property and all four are entirely within the control of the investor.

1. Choice of location and type of property.
2. Whether there is scope for adding value.
3. Whether borrowing is utilised.
4. Whether professional advisers are used.

Two examples are provided on pages 23–25 and 27–29 to illustrate the process of buying a property for investment purposes and to indicate the returns an investor might anticipate. The first example involves the purchase of a three-bedroom house in Cambridge, while the second focuses on a two-bedroom flat in London. Both these examples assume the simplest scenario – that the properties are in immaculate order and are ready to let. In the case of the Cambridge property, part-furnishing is required, while the London property has been bought with curtains, carpets and white goods (ie fridge, cooker and washing machine) included in the purchase price. Both properties are bought for cash and buying agents are used to advise on the purchase of the property, to furnish it (in the case of the Cambridge property), and subsequently to let and manage it.

Examples 1 and 2 show the returns that an investor might well expect over five years when he buys a property in a reasonably good location using buying agents' assistance throughout. The projected increases in both capital and rental values provide an estimate of the profits that might well be anticipated assuming modest growth over the five-year period. Even with these conservative estimates, the returns are materially better than many other forms of investment. In addition, the investor has the satisfaction of owning the property. As will be seen in later chapters, these average returns can, in various ways, be dramatically increased.

The property investment process step by step

Examples 1 and 2 illustrate the various steps involved when investing in residential property. These include the following.

I. Acquisition costs

Acquisition costs include:

- stamp duty – currently 0 per cent on properties up to £60,000, 1 per cent up to £250,000, 1.5 per cent over £250,000 and 2 per cent on properties over £500,000
- solicitors' fees – as solicitors have become more competitive, these fees have become increasingly negotiable; however, for the purpose of the examples in this book, solicitors' fees are estimated at 1 per cent of the purchase price including all disbursements and VAT
- valuation/survey fees – a valuation/survey is advisable whether or not borrowing on the property, and is estimated here at 0.3 per cent of purchase price plus VAT.

2. Buying agent's fee

If a buying agent is used (see Chapter 2), then the average acquisition fee is likely to be in the region of 1.5 per cent of purchase price plus VAT.

3. Furnishing

The decision has to be made whether to fully furnish, part furnish or not furnish at all (see Chapter 6). If a buying agent is used to furnish the property, then budget on a fee of 12.5 per cent of the furnishing package plus VAT for advising on and organising this.

4. Letting and management

The property then has to be let and managed. If a buying agent or a letting and management company is used, then fees can vary between 10 per cent plus VAT per annum and 17.5 per cent plus VAT per annum (see Chapter 5).

The anticipated annual income before any expenses are deducted, when expressed as a percentage of the total acquisition costs, is known as the gross yield. The gross yield, often quoted by developers and estate agents, is a meaningless figure; what matters is the net income, which the investor receives after all expenses are deducted. This is called the net yield.

Most developers quote anticipated gross yields and some calculate such gross yields on the sale price of the property excluding acquisition costs and furnishings. This practice is at best confusing as it doesn't give the investor an accurate indication of the actual income he is going to receive. The only way to calculate the actual anticipated net income is to work out the net yield.

5. Insurance

Insurance of the property and the contents provided is an expense always payable by the landlord unless buildings insurance is included in the

(continues on page 26)

EXAMPLE 1

The purchase and letting of a house in Cambridge using a buying agent

This example deals with the purchase and letting of a freehold Victorian terraced house in Cambridge, which has three bedrooms and one bathroom.

In this example the assumptions are that:
- the house has been professionally and fully renovated prior to purchase
- a buying agent is used at every stage
- house prices in Cambridge increase at 5% pa over five years
- rental incomes in Cambridge increase at 5% pa over five years, and
- expenses increase at 5% pa over five years.

After five years, the **total pre-tax return** on capital invested is **11% pa net** (3.3% pa on capital plus 7.7% pa on income), as shown in the table below.

CAPITAL	Value of house after 5 years	Total acquisition costs over 5 years	Net capital gain	Percentage return pa
	£134,008	£115,183	£18,825	3.3%[1]

INCOME	Total rental income over 5 years	Total expenses over 5 years	Net income gain	Percentage return pa
	£44,430	£16,319	£28,111	7.7%[2]

1 *£18,825 as a percentage of £115,183 = 16.3%, and 16.3% ÷ 5 = 3.3% pa*
2 *£44,430 as a percentage of £115,183 = 38.6%, and 38.6% ÷ 5 = 7.7% pa*

More detailed analysis

Ⓐ Projection of acquisition costs and net income

Acquisition and refurbishment costs	£
Purchase price	105,000
Acquisition costs: legal fees, stamp duty, valuation fees (an estimated 3.5% + VAT)	4,318
Buying agent's fee (1.5% + VAT)	1,851
Part-furnishing package (ie carpets, curtains and white goods only)	3,500
Project management fee (12.5% of part-furnishing package + VAT)	514
Total costs	**£115,183**

Letting income
Let @ £950 pcm but allowing 1 month void pa = £10,450 pa
Gross yield = 9.1% pa

Less the following annual maintenance costs:	£
Letting and management fee (15% + VAT)	1,842
Insurance	300
Statutory inspections	150
Garden maintenance	100
Allowance for general maintenance	300
Tax return work	120
Total expenses	**£2,812**

Total anticipated net income = £7,638 pa
Net yield = 6.6% pa

Ⓑ Projection of return on capital invested

Assuming that capital and rental values each grow by 5% pa over the five-year period, capital and income growth projections are as follows.

Capital growth
This is based on £105,000 and not the total cost figure of £115,183, as the value of property when bought is £105,000 and not £115,183.

Compound growth at 5% on £105,000:
Year 1   105,000   +   5,250   =   £110,250
Year 2   110,250   +   5,512   =   £115,762
Year 3   115,762   +   5,788   =   £121,550
Year 4   121,550   +   6,077   =   £127,627
Year 5   127,627   +   6,381   =   £134,008

New value after 5 years   =   £134,008

The total acquisition and refurbishment costs are £115,183. After five years, furnishings are depreciated to nil and the total acquisition costs of £6,169 (legal fees, stamp duty, acquisition fee etc) are written off in Year 1.

Net capital gain is therefore £134,008 less £115,183 = £18,825. When expressed as an increase on total costs of £115,183, the net capital gain is 16.3% or, when apportioned over five years, it is 3.3% pa.

Income growth
This is based on the anticipated net income figure of £7,638. It assumes that the annual expenses deducted of £2,812 also increase by 5% pa (totalling £16,319 over five years).

Compound growth at 5% on £7,638:
Year 1   7,638   +   382   =   £8,020
Year 2   8,020   +   401   =   £8,421
Year 3   8,421   +   421   =   £8,842
Year 4   8,842   +   442   =   £9,284
Year 5   9,284   +   464   =   £9,748

Total income over 5 years   =   £44,315

So, total acquisition and refurbishment costs are £115,183, while total income over five years is £44,315. This income apportioned over five years gives a figure of £8,863 pa, while income growth is 7.7% pa.

Total return
Therefore the total return over five years is **3.3% pa capital growth + 7.7% pa income growth**, which gives an **11% pa pre-tax return** on capital invested.

service charge of a flat, in which case the tenant pays. In these circumstances, however, the landlord still pays for contents insurance in respect of the contents provided.

6. Statutory inspections
There are a number of statutory inspections that have to be made each year to comply with current legislation (see Chapter 5).

7. Garden maintenance
In theory tenants should be made responsible for garden maintenance costs, but in practice in the case of a typical terraced house there will be some garden maintenance that the landlord will have to pay for.

8. General maintenance
Maintenance of a property will be minimal if the property has been comprehensibly refurbished and is in immaculate order. Maintenance of new properties should be negligible. For either type of property we have allowed a figure of £300 per annum (£350 per annum for London). This figure includes miscellaneous expenditure such as inventory charges and responsibility for Council Tax during any brief periods when the property is without tenants.

9. Accountants' fees
It is necessary to include full details of income and expenditure from the investment property on the investor's tax return and a figure of £120 has been allowed for additional work carried out by the landlord's accountant.

10. Capital and income growth
Capital growth and income growth depend on a multitude of factors which are considered in detail in this book. For illustrative purposes only, capital and income growth have each been assumed at 5 per cent each year for the house in Cambridge and at 6.5 per cent each year for the flat in London.

The two examples provided in this chapter assume that the properties are bought for cash. In practice most investors buy with the assistance of a mortgage because either they have insufficient cash resources to buy the property outright or because they wish to borrow. If a mortgage is to be utilised, then a provisional mortgage offer should always be obtained before making an offer on a property.

The actual mechanics of buying a residential property for investment purposes are in fact quite straightforward. What matters is choosing the right property, making the right improvements or

(continues on page 30)

EXAMPLE 2

The purchase and letting of a flat in London using a buying agent

This example outlines the purchase and letting of a flat in Chelsea, London SW3, with two bedrooms, one bathroom and one shower room. The flat has a 78-year lease, a share of the freehold and car parking. It is in a purpose-built block (1970s) with 24-hour porterage.

The assumptions are that:
- the flat has been professionally and fully renovated
- the flat is being sold with new curtains, carpets and white goods
- a buying agent is used at every stage
- flat prices in London SW3 increase at 6.5% pa over five years
- rental incomes in London SW3 increase at 6.5% pa over five years, and
- expenses increase at 6.5% pa over five years.

After five years, the **total pre-tax return** on capital invested is **11.8% pa net** (5.2% pa return on capital plus 6.6% pa return on income), as shown in the table below.

CAPITAL	Value of house after 5 years	Total acquisition costs over 5 years	Net capital gain	Percentage return pa
	£393,000	£312,331	£81,568	5.2%[1]

INCOME	Total rental income over 5 years	Total expenses over 5 years	Net income gain	Percentage return pa
	£102,545	£49,199	£53,346	6.6%[2]

1   *£81,568 as a percentage of £312,331 = 26.1%, and 26.1% ÷ 5 = 5.2% pa*
2   *£102,545 as a percentage of £312,331 = 32.8%, and 32.8% ÷ 5 = 6.6% pa*

More detailed analysis

Ⓐ Projection of acquisition costs and net income

Acquisition and refurbishment costs	£
Purchase price	295,000
Acquisition costs: legal fees, stamp duty, valuation fee (an estimated 3.5% + VAT)	12,132
Buying agent's fee (1.5% + VAT)	5,199
Total costs	**£312,331**

Letting income
Let @ £525 per week but allowing 1 month void pa = £25,025 pa
Gross yield = 8.0% pa

Less the following annual maintenance costs:	£
Letting and management fee (15% + VAT)	4,411
Service charge	2,824
Contents insurance	220
Statutory inspections	190
Allowance for general maintenance	350
Tax return work	120
Total expenses	**£8,115**

Total anticipated net income = £16,910 pa
Net yield = 5.4% pa

Ⓑ Projection of return on capital invested

Assuming that both capital and rental values each grow by 6.5% pa over the five-year period, capital and income growth projections are as follows.

Capital growth
This is based on the purchase price of £295,000 less the estimated value of furnishings, etc @ £7,500 = £287,500.

Compound growth at 6.5% on £287,500:

Year 1   287,500   +   18,687   =   £306,187
Year 2   306,187   +   19,902   =   £326,089
Year 3   326,089   +   21,196   =   £347,285
Year 4   347,285   +   22,574   =   £369,859
Year 5   369,858   +   24,041   =   £393,900

New value after 5 years   =   £393,900

The total acquisition costs are £312,331. Furnishings are depreciated to nil over five years and the total acquisition costs of £17,331 (legal fees, stamp duty, acquisition fee etc) are written off in Year 1.

Net capital gain therefore is £393,900 less £312,331 = £81,569. When expressed as an increase on total costs of £312,331, the net capital gain is 26.1% or, when apportioned over five years, it is 5.2% pa.

Income growth
This is based on the anticipated net income figure of £16,911. It assumes that the annual expenses deducted of £8,114 also increase by 6.5% pa (totalling £49,199 over five years).

Compound growth at 6.5% on £16,911:

Year 1   16,911   +   1,099   =   £18,010
Year 2   18,010   +   1,171   =   £19,181
Year 3   19,181   +   1,247   =   £20,428
Year 4   20,428   +   1,328   =   £21,756
Year 5   21,756   +   1,414   =   £23,170

Total income over 5 years =   £102,545

So, total acquisition costs are £312,331, while total income over five years is £102,545. This income apportioned over five years gives a figure of £20,509 pa, while income growth is 6.6% pa.

Total return
Therefore the total return over five years is **5.2% pa capital growth + 6.6% pa income growth,** which gives an **11.8% pa pre-tax return** on capital invested.

alterations to that property, and letting the property to the right tenants. If buying agents and/or a letting and management company are used, then it is essential to choose the right firm.

Once the property is furnished and fully let it can be described as an 'up and running' investment and this is an increasingly readily saleable asset. A property that has already been furnished and let has had all the work done and has proved its suitability for rental. Increasingly, therefore, there is demand from other investors to buy 'up and running' investment properties. This has always been the case with commercial property. A fully let office building will almost always command a higher price than an empty office building for the simple reason that the majority of purchasers of office buildings are buying for investment, with the occupiers usually being the tenant rather than the owner.

Until about two years ago valuers were tending to discount residential properties that were let by an average of 5 per cent to 7.5 per cent of their open market value. This discount has now disappeared and there are indications that valuers are starting to reflect the increasing demand for 'up and running' investments by sometimes even adding a small premium to the valuations for such properties.

As we will see in Chapter 2, maximising returns from investment in residential property hinges primarily on adding value, then selling the 'up and running' investment and re-investing. The rapidly increasing demand for 'up and running' investments therefore makes this strategy entirely practical.

SUMMARY

◆ Anticipated capital and income returns from direct investment in residential property are likely to exceed many other investment options.

◆ Owning residential property allows total control over the investment by the owner.

◆ Investing in property satisfies a strong instinct to own land and property.

◆ Owning an investment property creates a business and profits can be substantially enhanced by adding value and 'gearing up'.

◆ We are currently in the early stages of the formation of a recognised and regulated residential investment market; returns from a correctly chosen residential property are likely to exceed many other forms of investment over the coming years.

CHAPTER 2

How to invest in residential property

Having established that investing in residential property is an appealing idea from a financial point of view as well as a personal satisfaction point of view, the next stage is to decide how to go about it. Three initial questions usually need to be answered.

- What type of property should be bought?
- Where should one buy the property?
- How does one identify the best opportunities?

In order that these questions can be answered satisfactorily, two important factors need to be considered first of all.

1. The amount of money available for investment.
2. The extent to which the investor wishes, or is able, to participate in the purchase and management process.

In addition, when buying a property for investment purposes there has to be a dominant motive.

- Is the property being bought as an investment? (It can always be sold at a later date and the proceeds invested in a house which the investor wishes to occupy.)
- Alternatively, is the property being bought primarily for occupation by the investor within a fairly short time-scale – perhaps two or three years?

The property should, ideally, be bought purely for investment purposes rather than being one in which the investor wishes to live one day. This is because when buying for investment reasons, a totally objective approach is required to maximise both capital growth and rental income returns. If occupation at some stage is the dominant motive, then investment returns have to be secondary.

So, the investor must decide at the outset which is the dominant motive. If equal priority is given to both motives, then this usually results in neither objective being satisfactorily achieved. However, as we will see later, when choosing to buy purely for investment, it is important that the property is also suitable for owner-occupation by third parties when it is eventually sold in the future.

Making some choices

With this advice in mind, there are five important questions that the investor has to consider, then answer, before taking the first steps towards buying a property for investment.

1. What amount of money is available?

How much money does the investor wish to commit to the investment, either with or without borrowing?

2. A flat or a house?

Is there a particular preference to buy a flat or a house?

3. Location?

Assuming that the dominant motive is to buy for investment purposes only and not to live in the property at a future date, does the investor mind where the property is? For example, if the investor has a top investment limit, with or without borrowing, of £85,000, then it would probably make more sense to buy a top quality two-bedroom, two-bathroom flat in a prime location in Oxford, Cambridge or Edinburgh rather than a poorly located one-bedroom or studio flat in London. Income returns will almost certainly be higher and a well located, top quality two-bedroom flat is likely to increase in value faster than a poorly located one-bedroom or studio flat in London.

4. Should buying agents be used?

Does the investor wish to use buying agents who will provide a selection of recommended properties, advise on the respective merits of each recommended property, and handle, if required, all aspects of the transaction? Is there a selection of buying agents available in the city or town chosen for investment?

5. Going it alone?

If there are no buying agents in the chosen city or town, or the investor has decided to buy an investment property without the assistance of a buying agent, how does he go about identifying the best opportunities?

Let's consider these points one by one.

What amount of money is available?

How much of the investor's cash resources and/or borrowing power he chooses to invest in residential property as opposed to other investment mediums has to be a personal decision by the investor. It will depend on his circumstances and his belief in the attractions of residential property as opposed to other forms of investment.

The prudent investor will always keep a reasonable reserve of around 25 per cent of his savings in a bank, building society or another quickly realisable savings account. An alternative way of looking at this is that he should keep 25 per cent of his borrowing power in reserve. This 25 per cent reserve is then available on those occasions when capital is tied up. For example, if the investor has a well-chosen residential investment property in a good location and he needs to sell it in order to realise some capital, he will always find a buyer whatever the state of the market. However, even in a very buoyant market, sales of investment property can take time, particularly when purchasers withdraw at the eleventh hour and the property has to be put back on the market.

As in all matters financial, the best test to gauge the amount of money available is to consider what amount of capital and/or borrowing the individual feels comfortable with investing. Overstretching oneself could lead to unnecessary anxiety. It could also result in the need to cut back on the quality of refurbishment or furnishing and equipping the property, which could seriously prejudice the performance of the investment property. (For further advice on borrowing, see Chapter 4.)

For those people who have completely or largely paid off the mortgage on the house that they occupy, it is totally unnecessary to have any spare cash to invest in residential property. Such people are often in their fifties and by providing a bank or building society with a first charge on their own property as well as a first charge on the property being purchased, they can purchase an investment in property without providing any money themselves. In these particular circumstances, the investment strategy is geared to net capital gains with income doing no more than covering outgoings. As 100 per cent of the total costs of the investment property will be borrowed, the investor will be looking for a high yielding property to cover the mortgage payments. Such a property held for 10 years until the investor is in his late sixties should, however, provide a substantial capital gain, which could considerably enhance his financial position in retirement.

A flat or a house?

For investment purposes, the ideal investment across the United Kingdom is either a one- or two-bedroom flat or a three- or four-bedroom house, centrally located in a city or town with a proven strong letting market. Ideally, the property should have private car parking. If it doesn't, close proximity to public transport is essential.

Some investors have an individual personal preference to buy either a flat or a house for investment. In fact, there is no reason why one type of property should perform better than the other, as the performance of each type of property depends on the amount paid and the location. In practice, the choice of buying a flat or a house is often clarified by the amount of money available for the purchase and the location chosen.

Studio flats should be ruled out entirely for investment purposes as there is always a more limited demand for such flats from investors and occupiers, and historically they have not performed as well as other property types. Generally speaking, basement flats should be avoided. In today's security-conscious world many purchasers, both owner-occupiers and investors, are put off by the increased security risk of lower ground floor flats (and sometimes ground floor flats too). In addition, don't consider any flat on the fourth floor or higher that is not served by a lift as this type of property is also less in demand.

Before purchasing a flat, the service charge needs to be carefully considered. Find out what the current service charge is and whether there is a sufficient sinking fund held by the freeholders of the block. A sinking fund is a reserve of money built up to cover all expected large capital expenditures (for example, replacing the roof). If the fund has accrued sufficiently it means that an investor purchasing a flat in the block will not be charged any large one-off payments to cover repairs. Establishing whether the sinking fund is sufficient or not requires a comparison of the extent of past and future repair work with the size of the fund, and it may be advisable to seek professional advice from a buying agent for this.

It is usually safer all round to purchase a flat in a purpose-built block rather than a conversion of an older house. Conversions can make excellent investments, but the greatest care should be taken to investigate the quality of the conversion, particularly if it was carried out more than 10 to 15 years ago, and what the maintenance charges incorporated in the service charge are likely to be over the coming years.

With all flats, the first point to check is whether there is any restriction on letting. This condition was quite commonly imposed by developers in the 1960s and early 1970s, and it is the first question that should be answered before incurring too much time and expense in appraising the property.

Particular care should be exercised if buying a flat for investment that is situated over a parade of shops. Some lenders simply will not lend on flats situated over commercial premises. Generally speaking, such flats do not perform as well from a capital growth point of view as purely residential blocks. Flats situated on any floor above a restaurant should be avoided altogether. The restaurant might currently be a fashionable, top quality one, but restaurants come and go, and it could be a very different sort of restaurant in two years' time.

Short leases should also be avoided. Only flats with a minimum of 65 years left to run on their lease should be considered by the potential investor. Making a success of buying properties with short leases requires considerable market knowledge and expertise and is best left to professional investors.

Given the choice, most people would prefer to buy a house rather than a flat for investment purposes. In fact, a three-bedroom house with one or two bathrooms is, in many ways, one of the best investment opportunities. In addition, most people feel that, because the freehold (or a share of the freehold) on a house is owned, there is a level of control over the investment which is rarely available with a flat.

Houses also offer the flexibility of being suitable for either single occupancy lets or for sharers – either young professionals or students (see Chapter 5). While there is a market for sharers to rent flats, particularly in London, the increase in the net income over a single occupancy let is usually considerably greater in the case of a house rather than a flat.

Victorian or period houses provide the greatest scope for adding value (see Chapter 3), but new or modern three-bedroom houses are also an attractive proposition. Most new or nearly new properties have low maintenance costs. In addition, they usually come with the National House Building Council's (NHBC) 10-year guarantee. The NHBC was set up over 60 years ago to help the house building industry construct good quality new homes by registering house builders, setting standards of construction, inspecting homes and promoting better building practices among house builders throughout the United Kingdom. The NHBC's Building Warranty indicates that the property has been built to acceptable standards and has been regularly inspected during construction by an NHBC officer. This warranty provides a structural guarantee on all new homes that are part of the scheme for a 10-year period.

The disadvantages of a house compared to a flat are that maintenance costs can be higher, particularly if the house was built pre-Second World War and has a large garden. Also, houses do not offer the same level of security as, for example, a flat in a modern block with 24-hour porterage.

Location?

If the main reason for purchasing a residential property is as an investment, then the property can be in any good location. Equally, from an investment performance point of view, it should make no difference whether the city or town chosen is well known to the investor or not provided that he takes the advice of a reputable buying agent or carefully researches the property and rental market of the area himself.

Many investors do, however, have a preference for a particular city, either because they are convinced that, for example, London is likely to show better capital growth than anywhere else, or because they have a particular liking and knowledge of a city having lived there at one time or perhaps attended university there.

London: its advantages and disadvantages

London is, of course, the biggest investment market with a wide choice of properties. As of early 1998, there is a huge amount of new development in London. This is primarily for investor purchasers and is in Docklands and EC postcodes. There is an acute danger of overdevelopment in these locations and up to the turn of the century investors should avoid these locations. Instead, they should concentrate on the traditional prime locations of SW1, SW3, SW7 and Mayfair where there is always a shortage of quality stock and capital values are likely to continue to lead the market. If these prime locations are out of reach financially, then the safest areas in terms of the strength of the letting market and the potential for capital growth are Earls Court, Maida Vale and Fulham. These three locations still offer value for money (particularly the first two locations), are well located, should experience above average capital growth and have extremely strong letting markets.

Historically, London has shown the greatest capital gains during times of economic boom, but has also shown the biggest falls in value during any slump. The exaggerated swings in value have been particularly marked in fringe locations such as Docklands. Another disadvantage of London generally is the amount of capital required for an investment and, compared to other top investment locations in the United Kingdom, the comparatively low income returns in terms of net yield on capital invested.

If the decision is made to invest in London, then around £100,000 is the minimum sum required to purchase and furnish a one-bedroom flat in a good location that is likely to show good capital and rental growth. To purchase a similar two-bedroom flat will require a minimum of around £160,000. The minimum sum required to purchase a quality three-bedroom house in London is around £200,000, with £300,000 being a more realistic minimum to get into the better areas with real growth potential.

Whether an investor chooses to buy a flat or a house in London, it is essential to maximise its appeal to tenants. In particular, it is extremely important to ensure that:

- the property is within a 15-minute – and preferably a 10-minute – walk of a tube station
- the property is well presented in terms of repair, decoration and furnishings. Tenants in London are, generally, highly selective – much more so than in other cities – and will only rent properties that really appeal to them.

Top 10 locations outside London

If an investor chooses not to buy in London, then the following 10 cities currently represent the best locations for investment in residential property:

- Aberdeen
- Bath
- Brighton
- Bristol
- Cambridge
- Edinburgh
- Glasgow
- Nottingham
- Oxford, and
- Reading.

All these cities have extremely strong rental markets and offer a combination of high income yields with excellent prospects for above average capital growth. Like any investment, the property bought must be easy to sell at any time in the future, and properties located in London, Edinburgh, Cambridge or Oxford in particular will usually attract a larger number of potential purchasers when offered for sale. These cities are the recognised and established favourites of foreign investors, particularly from the Far East, and are also popular with the large worldwide expatriate community who are constant buyers of property for investment.

There are, of course, numerous other towns and cities within the United Kingdom where investment in residential property will work extremely well. Even in a location where property values are currently stagnant and are unlikely to show much real growth in the foreseeable future, there may be a strong rental market (for example, Manchester). By purchasing properties with scope for adding value in such locations (see Chapter 3), higher returns can be achieved thus making these properties a better investment than an ordinary two-bedroom flat in a fashionable part of central London that has no scope for adding value. In fact, where there are opportunities to add value – as long as the location has a strong letting market – any city, town or even village in the United Kingdom can be the right location.

What these locations will not provide is such a ready market for investor purchasers who will concentrate mainly on London and the top 10 locations listed previously. This means that when the time comes to sell such a property, the investor will be reliant primarily on the owner-occupier market to purchase the property rather than investors. While he may sell the property quickly to an owner-occupier at maximum price, it becomes a safer proposition all round if the property being sold appeals to both owner-occupiers and investors.

The most convenient way to check comparable capital values throughout the United Kingdom is the quarterly index published by the Halifax Building Society. This index gives one of the most comprehensive and clearly laid out summaries of comparable house prices throughout the country (see Useful Addresses). As an example, at the end of the fourth quarter of 1997 average prices of similar semi-detached houses for Greater London and the top 10 locations outside London were as follows:

- London   £193,800
- Edinburgh   £109,600
- Reading   £105,100
- Oxford   £103,550
- Cambridge   £100,350
- Aberdeen   £85,000
- Brighton   £80,200
- Bath   £73,650
- Glasgow   £66,450
- Bristol   £64,050
- Nottingham   £51,500

Source: *Halifax Building Society except for figures for Oxford, Brighton and Bath, which have been compiled following a survey of estate agents by the author*

In addition to the quarterly reports published by the Halifax Building Society, another useful guide to capital values as well as rental values and yields is the Joseph Rowntree Foundation Index of Rents and Yields (see Useful Addresses).

Should buying agents be used?

Before assessing the pros and cons of using professional advisers it may be useful to define the roles of the various professionals and agents involved in the selling and buying process. These are:

- estate agents
- buying agents, and
- letting and management companies.

Estate agents

Estate agents are firms that sell property. An estate agent may be unqualified, or may be a fellow or associate of the National Association of Estate Agents (NAEA). Other estate agents may be members of the Royal Institute of Chartered Surveyors (RICS) or of the Incorporated Society of Valuers and Auctioneers (ISVA). The latter category offers estate agency services along with surveying and valuation services, for which they are qualified. However, whether qualified or not, the fundamental point, which is of great importance, is that estate agents act purely for the sellers of property.

It is therefore surprising how many purchasers of property are under the illusion that estate agents are in the business of helping or advising them. Although, naturally, some estate agents are more helpful than others, their only duty of care is to the seller of the property and their job is to obtain a sale at the best price or in the shortest space of time, or both, regardless of the merits of the property. The reason why so many purchasers believe that estate agents are acting on their behalf is because of their helpful and seemingly caring attitude. But this is simply sales talk. Usually there is no attempt to give the purchaser any genuine advice. Indeed, why should there be?

It is a surprising fact that the vast majority of purchasers of residential property take no independent advice before making what is usually by far the largest financial transaction of their lives. The reasons for this are threefold.

1. Owner-occupiers are usually certain about what they want and are happy to make up their own minds about purchasing a particular house and how much they want to pay for it.
2. Many purchasers wrongly rely on the advice given by estate agents who, as we have seen, are acting for the seller.
3. Purchasers are either unaware that there are specialist firms acting only for buyers of property called buying agents or, if they are aware of such firms, decide that they would prefer not to pay a buying agent's fee.

Buying agents
Buying agents are firms that specialise in acting purely for the purchaser of a property. Such agencies have been big business in the United States for many years. In the United Kingdom they were virtually unheard of until the late 1980s when a handful of specialist buying agents was established, primarily to advise wealthy purchasers who did not want the hassle and publicity involved in looking for expensive houses themselves. Gradually, the idea caught on and further buying agency firms were established to identify houses in all price ranges for occupation in many parts of the country. Several such firms, for example, set up in the West Country to advise purchasers on retirement homes. This service proved useful to people living in a different part of the country and saved both time and money in making long journeys to view totally unsuitable properties. These buying agencies (or home search agencies as they are sometimes called) have continued to multiply during the 1990s, most of them catering for people wishing to purchase properties for their own occupation.

In addition, a number of the large estate agent firms have set up their own buying or home search arms. These act for the purchaser and charge the purchaser a fee for their services. The drawback to these buying arms of large firms of estate agents is that while all the reputable agents would only charge a fee to either the buyer or the seller, not to both, there is an obvious temptation for the buying arm to recommend properties that the estate agency side of their business has been instructed to sell. This takes away the total impartiality of the buying arm of large estate agents. Prospective clients should therefore ensure that the properties recommended by a buying arm of an estate agent are not currently offered for sale through the agent itself. If they are, while the property recommended might be suitable and fairly priced, the purchaser should be aware of the incestuous nature of the transaction and be on his guard.

Buying agents specialising in investment property

The types of buying agent referred to in the previous section primarily act for occupier-purchasers. Their services are limited to assessing suitable opportunities according to their client's instructions and presenting them to the client for consideration. However, in the early 1990s a number of buying agencies were set up that specialise in acting for purchasers of property for investment purposes as opposed to occupation. These buying agents provide a comprehensive package service, if required, including refurbishment, furnishing, letting and management, and arranging finance.

Buying agencies specialising in investment property have multiplied steadily throughout recent years. This has been in response to demand from increasing numbers of investors wishing to purchase residential property. Primarily, these investors are either resident overseas or they are resident in the United Kingdom but have decided that they would prefer independent advice on buying an investment property with a full associated package service. (See Useful Addresses for a list of buying agents specialising in investment property.)

Some buying agencies specialising in investment property that have set up over the last two or three years (particularly in London) are small operations, often consisting of just one agent and a secretary. While they do handle the identification of the right property to purchase, they subcontract most and sometimes all of the other functions including refurbishment, furnishing, and letting and management. There is a clear danger here that the control and responsibilities are spread over a number of different organisations, often without the knowledge of the client.

A fundamental part of the success of investing in residential property is the performance of the property in terms of producing a constantly high rate of income. This is more likely to be achieved if the buying agent is also responsible for letting and management as he will have the responsibility for ensuring that the property he has recommended does perform in rental terms in the way that he originally projected.

It is important that the investor should obtain a clear answer in response to whether the buying agent subcontracts letting and management or whether he handles it in-house. If the buying agent subcontracts both the letting and the management, then it may be preferable to approach a letting and management company direct as opposed to arranging the letting and management through the buying agent. Unlike buying agents, virtually every town and city in the United Kingdom has several letting and management companies to choose from. A satisfactory option is if the buying agent subcontracts only the letting of the property (because, for example, there is a particularly strong local letting agent in the location where the property is being bought) but will be undertaking the management in-house. In the case of London, it is also worth bearing in mind that even the biggest and most professional buying agents cannot provide a highly effective letting service over the whole of the city, so they may in fact be able to provide their client with a better service by subcontracting the letting to a local specialist letting company.

Selecting the right buying agent
The most important part of the buying agent's service is, of course, identifying the right investment property. A good buying agent will know the particular area in which he operates in detail and will recommend only those properties that he knows are going to perform well from a rental point of view as well as showing better-than-average capital growth. He will also ensure that the property is bought at the most attractive price. It may seem to be a contradiction that a buying agent will aim to buy at the lowest price for the client when the agent's fee is usually based on a percentage of the buying price. However, all the established and successful buying agents have built their reputations on performance and will genuinely try and buy the chosen property at the lowest price possible. The reason for this is because they rely mainly on recommendations rather than advertising to obtain their clients and so performance is the key to their success.

A buying agent is often in a better position to negotiate the lowest price than a private individual. Buying agents will be well known to the local estate agents as major buyers of residential property in the area. As a result, estate agents are more likely to recommend an offer from a buying agent who has a proven track record of performing (ie proceeding to a quick exchange of contracts) rather than a similar offer from a person who is unknown to the selling estate agent and who may or may not perform. Buying agents specialising in investment property only operate in certain cities. To provide an expert and specialised service it is essential that they have a high degree of local knowledge both in terms of the likely increases in capital values and the rental market. Currently, the cities in the United Kingdom that are best served by such firms are London and the top 10 cities outside London listed on page 39. For the investor living overseas or for those living in the United Kingdom who do not want to be, or cannot be, involved in the investment process, then using a buying agent to acquire and manage investment properties in one of these cities makes a lot of sense.

Approaching a buying agent

If the investor does decide to use a buying agent, the best advice is to approach at least three or four firms at the same time and, having explained your requirements, see how they each perform in identifying and presenting suitable opportunities. Ask them for two or three referees who can be contacted, preferably by telephone, to obtain confirmation of the quality of the service provided. If any buying agent is unable or unwilling to provide such referees, then he should not be used.

Most buying agents will provide a free initial service and fees are only payable on exchange of contracts on a property identified by them. If, as suggested, three or four buying agents are approached, a considerable amount of research can be carried out on behalf of the potential investor.

Having considered all the possibilities presented, the potential investor can then decide which is the most attractive opportunity presented by the different buying agents and also which of the buying agents offers the most comprehensive and complete package service. At that stage the investor can also make up his mind whether to use a buying agent at all, assuming of course that the buying agent has not already identified the property to be purchased.

Negotiating a buying agent's fee

The disadvantage of using buying agents is that they charge fees. As a guideline, these fees are generally:

- a purchase fee of 1.5 per cent plus VAT of the purchase price of the property
- a 12.5 per cent plus VAT project management fee in respect of the cost of any refurbishment required
- between 0.5 per cent and 1 per cent plus VAT mortgage sourcing fee
- a project management fee for arranging furnishing at 12.5 per cent plus VAT of the cost or, alternatively, a built-in profit margin on the cost, and
- an average of 15 per cent plus VAT of the annual gross income for letting and managing the property (which is the same as a letting and management company would charge).

The advantages of using good buying agents are considerable in that they:

● identify the best opportunities
● do all the work, and
● provide a complete package service.

Often by negotiating the lowest price on acquisition, buying agents will more than pay for themselves. Like all service industries, the standard of buying agents varies and the most important decision of all in identifying the best opportunity through a buying agent is to choose the right firm in the first place. By asking the right questions and by judging their initial (free) performance it should be apparent which of the agencies is likely to provide the investor with the best service.

It is not necessary to use all the services of a buying agency. As mentioned previously, the investor may choose to use an independent letting and management company. He may also decide to use the buying service of an agency but arrange furnishing himself, then use the agency to let the property, but subsequently manage it personally. However, as a first-time investor in residential property, there is clearly a lot to be said for using the right buying agent throughout the whole process. As will be seen later (Chapter 3), the most important way of enhancing capital and income gains from individual properties is by adding value and most investors will need a buying agent to handle this aspect, certainly for their first investment.

Letting and management companies

Letting and management companies do not sell property, but instead specialise purely in letting and management. They vary enormously in efficiency and guidelines for choosing the right company are set out in Chapter 5.

Some letting and management companies offer a buying arm themselves and it can be anticipated that more will do so in the future. Currently, however, few of them offer a complete package service. A selection of letting and management agents offering a buying service in London and the top 10 cities are listed in Useful Addresses.

Letting and management companies that offer a buying service in other cities and towns can be discovered by talking to each of the letting and management companies in the city or town chosen (most are listed in *Yellow Pages*).

The Association of Residential Letting Agents (Arla) also has a telephone hotline (see Useful Addresses), which can assist in identifying such letting and managing companies. However, there are still relatively few letting and management companies that offer the full package buying service provided by buying agents specialising in investment property.

Going it alone?

It is quite feasible to invest successfully in residential property without using a buying agent and thereby saving a considerable amount of money on fees. However, acting for yourself is not advisable if you live overseas or are unable, or unwilling, to research your chosen location properly and to spend a reasonable amount of time on the buying process.

For those people who do decide to go it alone, the rewards and the personal satisfaction can be considerable. This is illustrated in Examples 3 and 4 (see pages 47–49 and pages 51–53), which are based on Examples 1 and 2 in Chapter 1 (see pages 23–25 and pages 27–29). Examples 3 and 4 have been amended to show the increased returns on capital invested that can be achieved when buying agents are not used.

As can be seen from Examples 1 and 3, the total annual return over the five-year period increases from 11 per cent when a buying agent is employed, to 13.6 per cent when no buying agent is used. Similarly, in Examples 2 and 4, the total annual return over the five years increases from 11.8 per cent to 14.1 per cent. Obviously the savings would not be as large if professional services were partly used (for example, for letting of the property), but they would still be substantial.

Buying 'off plan'

One situation in which investors sometimes acquire property without using buying agents – and frequently without researching the market very fully, if at all – is buying direct from developers 'off plan', often before construction has even started. The idea here is that the developer will sell the property at a slight discount on its true market value prior to commencement of construction.

What must be realised is that the developer is prepared to give this discount because he is passing the risk from himself to the purchaser. In a rising market, the strategy of buying 'off plan' from developers, particularly in London, has proved to be very successful for investors. Indeed, this is probably still the most common way of purchasing for buyers from the Far East.

In certain locations, however, there are risks with this strategy. Assuming an average build period of a year, market conditions, particularly in London, can change fundamentally either upwards or downwards. The latter happened in 1989 in the Docklands area of London and many investors who bought 'off plan' suffered considerable losses. The other big danger with this strategy is that no one knows what the letting market in that location will be like in a year's time, especially considering there may be a large number of flats coming onto the market at the same time. Certainly for the first-time investor in residential property, this option should be pursued with caution.

(continues on page 50)

EXAMPLE 3

The purchase and letting of a house in Cambridge without using a buying agent

This example deals with the purchase and letting of a freehold Victorian terraced house in Cambridge, which has three bedrooms and one bathroom.

In this example the assumptions are that:
- the house has been professionally and fully renovated prior to purchase
- a buying agent is not used
- house prices in Cambridge increase at 5% pa over five years
- rental incomes in Cambridge increase at 5% pa over five years, and
- expenses increase at 5% pa over five years.

After five years, the **total pre-tax return** on capital invested is **13.6% pa net** (3.8% pa on capital plus 9.8% pa on income), as shown in the table below.

CAPITAL	Value of house after 5 years	Total acquisition costs over 5 years	Net capital gain	Percentage return pa
	£134,008	£112,818	£21,190	3.8%[1]

INCOME	Total rental income over 5 years	Total expenses over 5 years	Net income gain	Percentage return pa
	£55,005	£5,628	£49,377	9.8%[2]

[1]   £21,190 as a percentage of £112,818 = 18.8%, and 18.8% ÷ 5 = 3.8% pa
[2]   £55,005 as a percentage of £112,818 = 48.8%, and 48.8% ÷ 5 = 9.8% pa

More detailed analysis

Ⓐ Projection of acquisition costs and net income

Acquisition and refurbishment costs	£
Purchase price	105,000
Acquisition costs: legal fees, stamp duty, valuation fees (an estimated 3.5% + VAT)	4,318
Part-furnishing package (ie carpets, curtains and white goods only)	3,500
Total costs	**£112,818**

Letting income

Let @ £950 pcm but allowing 1 month void pa = £10,450 pa
Gross yield = 9.3% pa

Less the following annual maintenance costs:	£
Insurance	300
Statutory inspections	150
Garden maintenance	100
Allowance for general maintenance	300
Tax return work	120
Total expenses	**£970**

Total anticipated net income = £9,480 pa
Net yield = 8.4% pa

Ⓑ Projection of return on capital invested

Assuming that capital and rental values each grow by 5% pa over the five-year period, capital and income growth projections are as follows.

Capital growth

This is based on £105,000 and not the total cost figure of £112,818, as the value of property when bought is £105,000 and not £112,818.

Compound growth at 5% on £105,000:

Year 1	105,000	+	5,250	= £110,250
Year 2	110,250	+	5,512	= £115,762
Year 3	115,762	+	5,788	= £121,550
Year 4	121,550	+	6,077	= £127,627
Year 5	127,627	+	6,381	= £134,008

New value after 5 years   =   £134,008

The total acquisition and refurbishment costs are £112,818. After five years, furnishings are depreciated to nil and the total acquisition costs of £4,318 (legal fees, stamp duty etc) are written off in Year 1.

Net capital gain is therefore £134,008 less £112,818 = £21,190. When expressed as an increase on total costs of £112,818, the net capital gain is 18.8% or, when apportioned over five years, it is 3.8% pa.

Income growth
This is based on the anticipated net income figure of £9,480. It assumes that the annual expenses deducted of £970 also increase by 5% pa (totalling £5,628 over five years).

Compound growth at 5% on £9,480:

Year 1	9,480	+	474	= £9,954
Year 2	9,954	+	498	= £10,452
Year 3	10,452	+	523	= £10,975
Year 4	10,975	+	549	= £11,524
Year 5	11,524	+	576	= £12,100

Total income over 5 years =   £55,005

So, total acquisition and refurbishment costs are £112,818, while total income over five years is £55,005. This income apportioned over five years gives a figure of £11,001 pa, while income growth is 9.8% pa.

Total return
Therefore the total return over five years is **3.8% pa capital growth + 9.8% pa income growth**, which gives a **13.6% pa pre-tax return** on capital invested.

Choosing near or far?

The golden rule of going it alone is to choose a location that the investor can get to know well. The potential investor may live in Exeter but decide that Oxford, where he was at university, would be the best place to invest. In fact, this is a dangerous and impractical choice. He would do far better to research the local market in Exeter and buy on his doorstep. In his home town it will be far easier to research quickly and thoroughly the housing market and perhaps find an opportunity for adding value.

In London, good local knowledge of a specific area is even more important. London is made up of a considerable number of areas, each with entirely different property markets. Within those specific areas there are often wide variations in the desirability of a specific location, even down to which side of the street and which end of the street are the most sought after.

Personal knowledge is best

Many thousands of pounds hinge on identifying the right location as well as the right property, and the only safe way to proceed is to develop that knowledge of the locality yourself. Over a period of perhaps two to three months, time at weekends and evenings (for those with full-time jobs) must be devoted to looking at as many properties as possible and assessing values both in terms of capital and rental values. If the process does not interest you, don't do it! Instead use a buying agent or don't invest in property at all. Ultimately, to be successful in property investment it is essential to have a real interest in your chosen property market and to be determined to become a local expert.

Never allow yourself to think that local estate agents know more than you: by the time you have finished your research, a lot of them won't. Listen to as much advice as possible, learn as much as possible about the local property market, but then rely on your own instinct and intuition, not on other so-called expert opinions. If, six months after having made your first investment, you realise that you could have bought a better property, don't be put off; it's all part of the learning process. The property can be sold to another investor as an 'up and running' concern, and a new and better opportunity can then be identified.

Researching the chosen property market

If you decide not to use the services of a buying agent, it is vitally important that you thoroughly research the local market into which you have selected to buy. Set out to become an expert in local property values both from a capital and rental point of view. Talk to as many estate agents as possible, look at as many properties as possible, talk to

(continues on page 54)

EXAMPLE 4

The purchase and letting of a flat in London without using a buying agent

This example outlines the purchase and letting of a flat in Chelsea, London SW3, with two bedrooms, one bathroom and one shower room. The flat has a 78-year lease, a share of the freehold and car parking. It is in a purpose-built block (1970s) with 24-hour porterage.

The assumptions are that:
* the flat has been professionally and fully renovated
* the flat is being sold with new curtains, carpets and white goods
* a buying agent is not used
* flat prices in London SW3 increase at 6.5% pa over five years
* rental incomes in London SW3 increase at 6.5% pa over five years, and
* expenses increase at 6.5% pa over five years.

After five years, the **total pre-tax return** on capital invested is **14.1% pa net** (5.7% pa return on capital plus 8.4% pa return on income), as shown in the table below.

CAPITAL	Value of house after 5 years	Total acquisition costs over 5 years	Net capital gain	Percentage return pa
	£393,900	£307,132	£86,767	5.7%[1]

INCOME	Total rental income over 5 years	Total expenses over 5 years	Net income gain	Percentage return pa
	£129,286	£22,460	£106,826	8.4%[2]

1   *£86,767 as a percentage of £307,132 = 28.3%, and 28.3% ÷ 5 = 5.7% pa*
2   *£129,286 as a percentage of £307,132 = 42.1%, and 42.1% ÷ 5 = 8.4% pa*

More detailed analysis

Ⓐ Projection of acquisition costs and net income

Acquisition and refurbishment costs   **£**
Purchase price   295,000
Acquisition costs: legal fees, stamp duty, valuation fee
(an estimated 3.5% + VAT)   12,132
Total costs   **£307,132**

Letting income
Let @ £525 per week but allowing 1 month void pa = £25,025 pa
Gross yield = 8.1% pa

Less the following annual maintenance costs: **£**
Service charge   2,824
Contents insurance   220
Statutory inspections   190
Allowance for general maintenance   350
Tax return work   120
Total expenses   **£3,704**

Total anticipated net income = £21,321 pa
Net yield = 6.9% pa

Ⓑ Projection of return on capital invested

Assuming that both capital and rental values each grow by 6.5% pa
over the five-year period, capital and income growth projections are
as follows.

Capital growth
This is based on the purchase price of £295,000 less the estimated
value of furnishings, etc @ £7,500 = £287,500.

Compound growth at 6.5% on £287,500:
Year 1   287,500 + 18,687 = £306,187
Year 2   306,187 + 19,902 = £326,089
Year 3   326,089 + 21,196 = £347,285
Year 4   347,285 + 22,574 = £369,859
Year 5   369,859 + 24,041 = £393,900

New value after 5 years   = £393,900

The total acquisition costs are £307,132. Furnishings are depreciated to nil over five years and the total acquisition costs of £12,132 (legal fees, stamp duty etc) are written off in Year 1.

Net capital gain therefore is £393,900 less £307,132 = £86,768. When expressed as an increase on total costs of £307,132, the net capital gain is 28.3% or, when apportioned over five years, it is 5.7% pa.

Income growth
This is based on the anticipated net income figure of £21,321. It assumes that the annual expenses deducted of £3,704 also increase by 6.5% pa (totalling £22,460 over five years).

Compound growth at 6.5% on £21,321:

Year 1	21,321	+	1,386	=	£22,707
Year 2	22,707	+	1,476	=	£24,183
Year 3	24,183	+	1,572	=	£25,755
Year 4	25,755	+	1,674	=	£27,429
Year 5	27,429	+	1,783	=	£29,212

Total income over 5 years =   £129,286

So, total acquisition costs are £307,132, while total income over five years is £129,286. This income apportioned over five years gives a figure of £25,857 pa, while income growth is 8.4% pa.

Total return
Therefore the total return over five years is **5.7% pa capital growth + 8.4% pa income growth**, which gives a **14.1% pa pre-tax return** on capital invested.

as many letting and management companies as possible, and look at as many houses and flats available to rent as possible.

The property market is like any other market where some goods are overpriced, some are correctly priced and some are underpriced. The only way to spot the right opportunity, when acting for yourself, is to concentrate on one particular location; by doing this you will quickly develop a knowledge of local values and desirable specific locations. Most towns and cities have property supplements in the local newspaper, which provide an excellent overview of the market.

Always remember that estate agents are acting for the vendors and therefore will not feel obliged to find out or identify any drawbacks to the property being offered for sale. However, the fact that estate agents are motivated by sales commission and are usually more interested in a quick, clean sale rather than obtaining the last few thousand pounds for the vendor, can work to the investor's advantage. It is also worth bearing in mind that many estate agents employ young and relatively inexperienced negotiators who may have limited knowledge of market values and whose prime concern is to effect a quick sale.

Do not just visit estate agents who appear to be the most active or the most up-market. Often it is the smaller and less successful agents who have the best buys on their books as they tend to recommend offers at below full value in order to get a quick sale and early payment of their sales commission.

There is no reason at all why bargains cannot be found when acting for yourself, but it is imperative to look at as many properties as possible before making a decision on which one to actually purchase. To be really successful in investing in residential property, it is essential to develop an instinct and feel for the market, but this can be obtained surprisingly quickly.

Spotting a bargain

Having got a feel for local market conditions, the potential investor will naturally be excited by a property that definitely appears to be cheap (ie for no immediately obvious reason it is priced materially below what the potential investor thinks is the fair market value or, alternatively, the estate agent selling the property is describing it as 'a bargain'). However, be on your guard. There is always a reason for something being sold under current market value.

Sometimes obvious bargains are indeed just that, but on many occasions there is a reason for the property being marketed cheaply and that reason needs to be considered carefully before committing. Part of the buying agent's job is always to ascertain why a particular property appears to be relatively cheap, but when acting for yourself you are the one who needs to find out. Apart from those properties that offer the potential to add value (see Chapter 3), the most common situations in which properties can be acquired at genuinely low prices are sales due to any of the three Ds: debt, death or divorce.

Debt

The most obvious situation where a property is on the market at a bargain price is a repossession by a bank or building society. Whatever the state of the property market, there are always repossessions for sale and certainly they can sometimes be acquired at under market value. Contact all the main banks and building societies direct and ask them to provide information on repossessions in the chosen location. This is a much more effective route than trying to obtain information about repossessions from estate agents. Often, so-called 'Repossession Lists' that are advertised extensively in the national press are a waste of money as they merely list information obtained directly from banks and building societies, and once published this is out of date.

Banks and building societies have, by law, to advertise the fact that they have received an offer for a repossession and that they are intending to accept the offer if no better offer is received within a set period. Such advertisements are often buried in small print in local newspapers, but it is worthwhile checking these advertisements as a slightly higher offer may still represent a bargain price.

Some banks and building societies sell repossessions at auction and normally a forthcoming auction of a property in a particular town is advertised in the town's local newspaper. Buying at auction can result in bargain properties, but all the research, including the legal work, needs to be done prior to the day of the auction and the best advice is not to buy at auction until you have had the experience of buying at least one or two properties in the usual way.

Often an effective way of buying a property at a bargain price is to approach owners of unsold lots the day after the auction. Most properties have reserve prices and those properties that are not sold at auction have failed to reach the reserve. Quite frequently banks and building societies will sell under the reserve price, sometimes considerably so, the day after the auction. In these circumstances a normal time period can usually be negotiated before exchange of contracts to ensure that all enquiries and research is completed. There is a service run by the *Estates Gazette*, which gives full information on properties not sold at auction (see Useful Addresses).

Death

Properties being sold by relatives, executors or personal representatives of a deceased person are often available at attractive prices. This occurs particularly where there are a number of beneficiaries for whom achieving the maximum price for a property is less important than simply selling the property and dividing the proceeds. Generally there is less determination by this type of vendor to obtain the highest price. Quite frequently such properties provide scope for adding value, particularly if they have been occupied by an elderly person who has been unwilling or unable to maintain it.

Divorce

With well over one in three marriages in the United Kingdom now ending in divorce, houses and flats are frequently for sale as a result of a separation or divorce. As the parties involved, by definition, wish to make a fresh start, quite often they are keen to sell the original marital home as quickly as possible and move on to their new lives. Although sales through divorce or separation do not regularly throw up as many bargain opportunities as repossessions or sales by executors, these circumstances can explain why a property free of faults is being sold at a below market price.

When is a bargain not a bargain?

How does the investor acting for himself know what to pay for a particular property? Perhaps one of the biggest advantages that a private investor has in residential property is that there is rarely a 100 per cent certainty as to the correct market value of any one property, and this is particularly the case for older properties. If somebody is selling a 'one off' two-bedroom, one-bathroom flat in central London and they obtain six estimates of value from six different firms of estate agents, it is quite usual for the valuations to vary by between 10 per cent and 20 per cent. Therefore, to a limited extent, the value of any property is dictated as much by the price for which the vendor decides to sell it for as by any other reason.

It is also a fact that valuers employed by banks and building societies are often cautious. They can do their job efficiently and accurately when they are valuing a property in a street or in a block of flats where there are numerous other similar properties and a number of these regularly change hands. Under these circumstances, they have market evidence to assist their valuations and there is little doubt as to what the property is worth.

However, in 'one off' situations this is not the case. Indeed, in parts of London there are many successful property dealers who earn substantial incomes by buying and selling properties without spending any money on them at all and without relying on rising values. These dealers are simply taking advantage of the fact that the valuation of residential property is an imprecise science and there is often room for a marginal gain.

As we will see in Chapter 3, some situations such as structural defects can provide the best opportunities for adding value. However, if the property is being sold cheaply because of its type or its location, then it should not be bought. A typical example is a four-bedroom terraced house with only a small patio garden fronting on to a busy roundabout. Such a property is never going to appeal to a family despite the four bedrooms because it has no garden. In addition, environmentally it is in a position that can never be improved. Therefore such a property will always be cheap in relation to other comparable properties in better locations. It would be a mistake for an investor to calculate that the income return on capital would be high and therefore that it would be a good investment.

So, it is essential that any property bought for investment purposes is suitable in the long term both as an investment property and for owner-occupation. The owner-occupier market will always constitute a major proportion of potential buyers for a property, particularly in London, Edinburgh, Oxford or Cambridge. By excluding this sector of purchasers, the future saleability and therefore potential capital growth will, by definition, be limited.

Getting assistance from an estate agent

If you decide to invest in residential property without using a buying agent, meet as many of the local estate agents as possible and explain your needs to them. Although they are acting for the vendors, if you can strike up a good working relationship with one or two of them then they will at least take the trouble to notify you immediately a suitable property appears on their books.

There is also nothing to stop you agreeing to pay an estate agent an acquisition fee of, perhaps, 1 per cent if he informs you of a property that is for sale through another estate agent. Unfortunately, however, unless the property required is in a high price bracket or is identified quite early on, estate agents usually fail to perform under these circumstances. If you are lucky, though, it may work and so it is worth trying.

The way to keep an estate agent's interest in you personally is to emphasise the financial resources you have available and the fact that you can move quickly when the right property is identified. Even so, experience has shown that it is best to telephone an estate agent at least once if not twice a week to remind him of your interest and to remind him of what you are looking for.

Estimating future yields

The two pro formas that appear on pages 59 and 60 can be used as quick ready-reckoners when appraising different properties in order to estimate anticipated net yields. The first pro forma is for those who do

intend to use a buying agent. However, with this option, the buying
agent should present all recommended opportunities with a similarly
detailed appraisal which clearly shows what the anticipated net yield
is likely to be. The second pro forma is for those who have chosen to
invest in a property without employing a buying agent. The purpose of
these pro formas is to make sure that nothing is overlooked. The fees
listed in the first pro forma are the average fees charged by buying
agents, but of course it may be possible to negotiate lower fees than
those indicated.

As in the various examples provided throughout this book, it is best
to allow a void period of one month every year when calculating the
gross income, although every effort should be made to achieve 100 per
cent occupancy (see Chapter 5). The average letting fee is 10 per cent of
the first year's received income reducing to 7.5 per cent if the tenant
stays on for a second or subsequent years. The average management
fee is 5 per cent of the received income. Once again, though, these rates
vary and are usually negotiable.

As far as insurance is concerned, if the property concerned is a
flat then buildings insurance is normally incorporated in the service
charge and therefore allowance only needs to be made for contents
insurance in respect of items provided by the landlord. Statutory
inspections are explained in detail in Chapter 5. Garden maintenance
will depend on the individual circumstances. In the case of a flat
where there are communal gardens, this is normally incorporated in
the service charge. For a house, sometimes the tenants agree
to maintain the garden and sometimes the responsibility falls to
the landlord.

The allowance for general maintenance work assumes that the
property falls into one of these three categories.
● The property has been refurbished and is in immaculate condition
  when bought
● The property has been put into immaculate condition immediately
  after being purchased
● The property is new or nearly new.

In the case of older properties, there may be higher, ongoing
maintenance costs and so the estimated figure of £300 in the pro forma
may need to be adjusted.

Water rates are not included because in most cases the obligation
falls to the tenant rather than the landlord. The exception is when the
property is let as a shared house (ie to a number of individuals who
rent rooms). Under these circumstances, the water rates are normally
paid by the landlord. Similarly the responsibility to pay Council Tax
usually falls to the tenant. The exception is when the property is empty,
in which case the expense falls to the landlord.

(continues on page 61)

PRO FORMA 1

Using a buying agent

	£
Acquisition and refurbishment costs	
Purchase price	....
Acquisition costs: legal fees, stamp duty, valuation fees (an estimated 3.5% + VAT)	....
Property acquisition fee (1.5% + VAT)	....
Refurbishment costs (get quotes)	....
Project management fee for refurbishment (12.5% + VAT)	....
Furnishing package (part or whole – get quotes)	....
Total costs	....

Letting income

Let @ £ .... pcm but allowing 1 month void per year = £ .... pa

Gross yield = ... % pa (ie total anticipated letting income as a percentage of total costs)

Less the following annual maintenance costs:	£
Letting and management fee (15% + VAT)	....
Service charge (ie for a flat/maisonette)	....
Insurance (buildings/contents)	....
Statutory inspections	150
Garden maintenance	100
Allowance for general maintenance	300
Tax return work	120
Total expenses	....

Total anticipated net income = £ ....

Net yield = ... **% pa (ie total anticipated net income as a percentage of total costs)**

PRO FORMA 2

Not using a buying agent

Acquisition and refurbishment costs   £

Purchase price   ....

Acquisition costs: legal fees, stamp duty,
valuation fees (an estimated 3.5% + VAT)   ....

Furnishing/refurbishment package
(part or whole – get quotes)   ....

Total costs   ....

Letting income

Let @ £ .... pcm but allowing 1 month void per year = £ .... pa

Gross yield = ... % pa (ie total anticipated letting income as a
percentage of total costs)

Less the following annual maintenance costs: £

Service charge (ie for a flat/maisonette)   ....

Insurance (buildings/contents)   ....
Statutory inspections   150
Garden maintenance   100
Allowance for general maintenance   300
Tax return work   120

Total expenses   ....

Total anticipated net income = £ ....

**Net yield = ... % pa (ie total anticipated net income as
a percentage of total costs)**

SUMMARY

- ◆ Decide how much money you wish to invest in a property.

- ◆ Next, decide on the location and the type of property according to your budget.

- ◆ Then decide whether to use a buying agent, or the buying arm of an estate agent or letting and management company. This will depend on availability, circumstances and personal preference.

- ◆ If using a buying agent, approach as many as possible and ask lots of questions before making a decision as to which firm to use. Usually their advice is entirely free until you contract to buy a property recommended by them.

- ◆ Consider at least four or five properties recommended by the buying agent before making a final decision. Remember, there's always another opportunity!

- ◆ If you choose not to use a buying agent for any part of the investment process, then become an expert in your chosen location.

- ◆ Having followed the above advice, rely on your own instinct. Success in property investment, as in all things, requires faith in your own instinctive judgement!

CHAPTER 3

Adding value

The best known saying in the property world is that the three most important factors to consider when buying a property are: location, location, location. However, there are another three equally important factors that should be considered in order to achieve the best performance from property investment and they are: adding value, adding value, adding value.

It is true that location is very important, but adding value to a property in an average location will usually produce higher returns than relying on a good location alone. The best results of all are obtained from adding value to properties in the best locations.

The ability to add value to a property is a major advantage that property investment has over most other investment mediums. If you buy a share in a company, then you personally have no control over whether the share price goes up or down. That is dictated by the actions of the directors of that company and by movements of share prices generally on the financial markets. This lack of control applies both to dividends (ie income return) and to capital values. If you buy a work of art, a sculpture or a picture, you are reliant entirely upon capital growth to provide a return on investment. In that instance, capital growth is, once again, totally outside your control and is dependent on fashion and market forces.

The difference with property is that you personally are in control and can, by adding value, materially enhance both capital and income returns. As with other forms of investment, you cannot alter general price movements in the property market. Nevertheless, in a year when property prices across the country drop by an average of, for example, 5 per cent, you could easily increase the value of your particular property by 10 per cent by adding value and therefore still make a net gain of 5 per cent for that year.

Primarily, there are six ways of adding value to a residential property.
1. Buy a property in a 'special' location.
2. Buy a property requiring refurbishment.
3. Buy a property with scope for creating an extra bedroom in the roof space.

4. Buy a property with potential for an extension to the rear.
5. Buy a property with potential to create an additional plot for
    another house to the side or rear of the existing property.
6. Buy a plot of land with planning permission and then construct a
    new house.

The examples used in this chapter assume that buying agents are
used throughout to identify the right property, to obtain estimates for
and project manage the work, to furnish the property, and
subsequently to let and manage the property. It is essential that, if
buying agents are used, the firm chosen is capable of providing the full
package. Such a firm will, of course, be familiar with the methods of
adding value. The purpose of this chapter is to ensure that, even when
buying agents are used, the investor is in a position to ask all the right
questions and therefore to get a high quality service.

In the examples that follow, standard buying agents' fees have been
assumed throughout. However, an alternative way of maximising the
professional input of buying agents is to negotiate an agreed
percentage of the increase in value over the cost of adding value
instead of paying the standard acquisition and project management
fees. If this option is used, the increased net value will need to be
determined by an independent valuation on completion of the work.

Identifying a special location

A special location is where, for a specific reason, there will be a jump in
the value of a property in its existing state over a relatively short period
of time. The most readily available opportunities are existing houses
that adjoin or are close to a 'non-conforming use' that is about to be
redeveloped.

An example would be an average residential street in Cambridge, a
cul-de-sac, which has a haulage company at the end of the road
operating from a site of around 0.2 acres. These premises are unsightly
and also generate substantial noise and nuisance as lorries are
continually arriving and leaving the depot. These premises are put on
the market through estate agents and are advertised as being suitable
for residential redevelopment. A word with the local planning
authority will confirm whether the planners are keen to see the non-
conforming use demolished and redeveloped with new houses.

The best time to purchase an existing house in this street is the
moment that the haulage company site is put up for sale. From the
investor's enquiries with the local planning authority it is clear that the
site is going to be sold and redeveloped in the near future. Not only
will the non-conforming use disappear, but the new development will,
itself, lift the desirability and values of the other properties in the street.
In order to maximise gains, timing in this situation is crucial. If the

investor waits until planning permission has actually been granted for the new development, then some increase in values may already be reflected in the asking prices of surrounding houses. It is best, having ascertained that redevelopment is a virtual certainty, to buy an investment property while the non-conforming use is still in existence and continues to have the maximum depressing effect on values in the street.

The residential investment market is not sophisticated. Indeed why should it be as it consists, in the main, of owners buying and selling houses for the purpose of occupation and this generally has nothing to do with maximising on capital gain. Usually a house is up for sale because the owners are changing jobs, need a bigger or smaller house, or because of the three Ds: debt, death or divorce (see Chapter 2, pages 55–56). By comparison, in a sophisticated market run by professionals – for example, the stock market – values are constantly adjusted by professional buyers and sellers who take into account anticipated future events up to a year ahead. This is simply not the case with the residential property market where values are determined by current rather than future circumstances.

The way that the potential investor can spot these special situations is firstly to identify a non-conforming use that is for sale and then to look at any houses or flats that are for sale close by. Good buying agents will know of all such opportunities in their area and will notify their clients accordingly. If you choose not to use buying agents, then the commercial and residential property supplements of the local paper will advertise the sale of many such sites.

Assuming a static property market, one can expect that once the new residential development is completed there will be a jump in value of nearby houses to a market norm. To illustrate this, look back at Example 3 which appears in Chapter 2 (see pages 47–49). Let's assume that the house used in Example 3 is in an adjoining street to the cul-de-sac with a haulage company sited at the far end (as previously mentioned). The selling price of a fully refurbished, three-bedroom, one-bathroom Victorian house in the street in Example 3 is around £105,000. If a virtually identical property is on the market for £95,000 in the cul-de-sac with the non-conforming use, then it is clear that the cul-de-sac suffers from a discount of nearly 10 per cent due to the non-conforming use. Therefore it is a reasonable and safe assumption that, on completion of the new development, the £95,000 property will increase immediately by £10,000 to £105,000.

All we have done is identify an inferior location which we know is going to improve dramatically within a reasonably short time-scale. The redevelopment of the non-conforming use site has a significant effect on the estimated returns over a five-year period, as can be seen from Example 5 (see pages 67–69).

This example illustrates that the increase in value comes in Year 2 once the new residential development is completed. Total capital gain in that year is £14,987 comprising a £10,000 uplift in value and a 5 per cent average increase in property prices of £4,987.

This is roughly a £15,000 increase in value in one year and therefore to maximise returns it would make sense to sell the investment property at the end of Year 2 as an 'up and running' investment and reinvest the funds in another property where there is again scope to add value.

Holding the property for a further three years, as in this example, only produces the average capital growth as all the added value is achieved in Year 2.

Adding value with a refurbishment

While refurbishment may seem the most obvious way to add value, many people pay too much for refurbishment opportunities and/or underestimate the cost of the required refurbishment. For example, houses and flats that are advertised as being 'ideal for refurbishment' often sell for a higher price than they are worth to either potential occupiers or to investors and developers. While it is an occupier's privilege to pay too much for the house he wants to live in, it is certainly not the way to be an effective property investor.

Until the property investor has built up several years' experience, the best advice is to avoid the following refurbishment opportunities entirely:

- major refurbishments involving substantial expenditure, particularly when they are combined with the necessity for planning permission, for example the conversion of a house to flats
- refurbishment of basements flats that have been created by the conversion of older houses.

Both types of refurbishment invariably involve higher costs and longer time-scales than originally anticipated and are best left to professional builders or developers.

On the other hand, the most attractive (and indeed the most commonly encountered) refurbishment opportunities for investors are:

- flats requiring purely cosmetic improvements, for example a new bathroom, new kitchen and redecoration
- upgrading Victorian houses that are in sound condition but have had period features such as fireplaces and panelled doors removed or covered
- terraced houses that have settlement at the rear of the property or that have other structural problems.

(continues on page 70)

EXAMPLE 5

Adding value as a result of the redevelopment of an adjoining non-conforming use site

This example deals with the purchase and letting of a freehold Victorian terraced house in Cambridge, which has three bedrooms and one bathroom.

In this example the assumptions are that:
- the house has been professionally and fully renovated prior to purchase
- the house is in a cul-de-sac that has a haulage company based at the far end that is up for sale for redevelopment
- buying agents are used at every stage
- house prices in Cambridge increase at 5% pa over five years
- rental incomes in Cambridge increase at 5% pa over five years, and
- expenses increase at 5% pa over five years.

After five years, the **total pre-tax return** on capital invested is **13.9% pa net** (5.4% pa on capital plus 8.5% pa on income), as shown in the table below.

CAPITAL	Value of house after 5 years	Total acquisition costs over 5 years	Net capital gain	Percentage return pa
	£132,823	**£104,595**	**£28,228**	**5.4%**[1]

INCOME	Total rental income over 5 years	Total expenses over 5 years	Net income gain	Percentage return pa
	£44,315	**£16,319**	**£27,996**	**8.5%**[2]

1   *£28,228 as a percentage of £104,595 = 27%, and 27% ÷ 5 = 5.4% pa*
2   *£44,315 as a percentage of £104,595 = 42.4%, and 42.4% ÷ 5 = 8.5% pa*

More detailed analysis

Ⓐ Projection of acquisition costs and net income

Acquisition and refurbishment costs	£
Purchase price	95,000
Acquisition costs: legal fees, stamp duty, valuation fees (an estimated 3.5% + VAT)	3,907
Buying agent's fee (1.5% + VAT)	1,674
Part-furnishing package (ie carpets, curtains and white goods only)	3,500
Project management fee (12.5% of part-furnishing package + VAT)	514
Total costs	**£104,595**

Letting income
Let @ £950 pcm but allowing 1 month void pa = £10,450 pa
Gross yield = 10% pa

Less the following annual maintenance costs:	£
Letting and management fee (15% + VAT)	1,842
Insurance	300
Statutory inspections	150
Garden maintenance	100
Allowance for general maintenance	300
Tax return work	120
Total expenses	**£2,812**

Total anticipated net income = £7,638 pa
Net yield = 7.3% pa

Ⓑ Projection of return on capital invested

Assuming that capital and rental values each grow by 5% pa over the five-year period, capital and income growth projections are as follows.

Capital growth
This is based on £95,000 and not the total cost figure of £104,595, as the value of property when bought is £95,000 and not £104,595.

Compound growth at 5% on £95,000:

Year 1	95,000	+	4,750		=	£99,750
Year 2	99,750	+	4,987 + 10,000 increase in value		=	£114,737
Year 3	114,737	+	5,737		=	£120,474
Year 4	120,474	+	6,024		=	£126,498
Year 5	126,498	+	6,325		=	£132,823

New value after 5 years = £132,823

The total acquisition and refurbishment costs are £104,595. After five years, furnishings are depreciated to nil and the total acquisition costs of £5,581 (legal fees, stamp duty, acquisition fee etc) are written off in Year 1.

Net capital gain is therefore £132,823 less £104,595 = £28,228. When expressed as an increase on total costs of £104,595, the net capital gain is 27% or, when apportioned over five years, it is 5.4% pa.

Income growth
This is based on the anticipated net income figure of £7,638. It assumes that the annual expenses deducted of £2,812 also increase by 5% pa (totalling £16,319 over five years).

Compound growth at 5% on £7,638:

Year 1	7,638	+	382	=	£8,020
Year 2	8,020	+	401	=	£8,421
Year 3	8,421	+	421	=	£8,842
Year 4	8,842	+	442	=	£9,284
Year 5	9,284	+	464	=	£9,748

Total income over 5 years   £44,315

So, total acquisition and refurbishment costs are £104,595, while total income over five years is £44,315. This income apportioned over five years gives a figure of £8,863 pa, while income growth is 8.5% pa.

Total return
Therefore the total return over five years is **5.4% pa capital growth + 8.5% pa income growth,** which gives a **13.9% pa pre-tax return** on capital invested.

These particular examples are less obvious to purchasers than houses advertised as being 'ideal for refurbishment' and hence there is usually less competition for them. But in these instances, when bought at the right price, a considerable increase in capital value over and above the cost of the remedial work can be expected.

If buying agents are not being used, the best advice when taking on a refurbishment project is to deal directly with a good local builder. The downfall of many small refurbishment projects is using architects. Architects are essential for major development work such as building a new property or carrying out a substantial extension. However, for relatively minor refurbishment works, architects' fees will not only add materially to costs but often they will also advise works that do not add value.

A builder should be selected as the result of a recommendation and not from an advertisement or from just flicking through *Yellow Pages*. Ask local estate agents to recommend the most reliable and reasonably priced of the local builders. A good local builder will have carried out similar work and will be able to demonstrate that he has a real feel for property. Always get three quotations – not estimates – ensuring that all works are included in the agreed written specification. In addition, ask for two or three references from recent customers.

Having chosen the builder and accepted his quotation, only agree payment for works carried out at specified stages. On completion of the work, retain a minimum of 10 per cent of the quoted price against any remedial works that may be required in the first three months. If you have any doubts about the quality of the work during the refurbishment process, instruct an independent local surveyor at an agreed cost per hour to inspect the works and report back to you.

For minor refurbishments, the most cost-effective option is to act as the main contractor yourself employing the different trades required. However, for anything other than minor refurbishment works, this is best left until experience has been gained on two or three projects. Even with the experience of several projects, it is important to ensure that time is available for regular inspections of the work in progress.

The prices quoted by builders and other tradespeople will fluctuate enormously depending on how much they want the work and how much time they have spent on estimating the costs. Many small builders literally guess a price for the job rather than working it out stage by stage, and this invariably produces quotations that are much too high. Be sure, therefore, to obtain a minimum of three quotations, and make it absolutely clear to the builder or tradesperson that he is in a competitive situation and that you are looking for the keenest price.

It is essential to impress on each of the builders and tradespeople who tender for the work that you are 'in business' and are not going to pay over the odds. Never agree to pay for work on an hourly or time basis;

instead agree a fixed price for the work that you have clearly specified. Finally, builders always aim to make most of their profit on 'extras' (additional jobs that the client asks to be undertaken once work has started) when they are in effective control of pricing additional works. The way to avoid this is to be certain that all required works are included in the original specification.

Buying agents will, of course, take care of all these aspects of a refurbishment, and because they put a lot of work out to builders and tradespeople they are often able to obtain the most competitive quotes. However, with the right amount of time devoted to getting quotes from builders, there is no reason why anyone choosing to 'go it alone' cannot obtain equally competitive quotes.

Cosmetic improvements to a flat

The flat in Example 6 (see pages 73–75) is identical to Example 2 (see pages 27–29) in Chapter 1, but it is unmodernised and has the original bathroom and kitchen fittings dating back to the time of construction in the 1970s. The flat is badly presented and is unappealing. Discussions with local estate agents and with the porter at the block ascertain that a similar flat in immaculate order recently sold for £295,000 and so a cash purchase is agreed at £240,000.

Quotations are then obtained (prior to exchange of contracts) from tradespeople to carry out the following improvements:
- a new kitchen with new appliances
- a new bathroom with high quality tiles
- conversion of separate WC into a shower room with WC
- new panelled doors throughout with brass door furniture
- replacement of white plastic sockets and switches with brass fittings
- plaster coving to the reception room and main bedroom ceilings
- recessed spotlights installed into new false ceilings in the kitchen and main bathroom
- moulded beading to all existing bedroom cupboard doors to create panelled effect
- high-quality fitted carpets throughout or, alternatively, wooden flooring in main reception room, depending on preference
- plaster wall uplights in place of existing wall lights, and
- high quality redecoration throughout with quality curtains hung to all windows.

The most competitive quotations received from the tradespeople come to a total of £22,325. Just prior to the exchange of contracts, an eight-week completion period is negotiated with the vendor together with the right to have access between exchange and completion to carry out the agreed improvement works. Therefore, on completion of purchase the flat is ready for letting. The basically cosmetic refurbishment transforms the flat and increases its appeal dramatically. The effect the refurbishment has in terms of adding value is fully illustrated in Example 6.

As can be seen, the total return per annum increases from 11.8 per cent in Example 2 to 15.7 per cent in Example 6 as the result of the straightforward modernisation of the flat. The initial added value to the refurbishment of just over £11,000 (valuation on completion of all works at £295,000 less the total costs of £283,718) is realised immediately after completing the modernisation.

As with Example 5 outlining the house close to the haulage company (see pages 67–69), to maximise returns it would make sense to sell the flat as an up and running investment early on in the five-year period in order to switch into another situation with potential for adding value. There would be no point in switching into another property without scope for adding value as substantial sale and purchase costs would be incurred and capital growth, assuming a similar location, would be much the same.

Partitioning one large bedroom into two bedrooms

Occasionally, large one-bedroom flats appear on the market that will readily convert into two-bedroom flats. Such flats are usually conversions carried out some years ago when space was not at such a premium. Suppose the bedroom in a one-bedroom flat is a large double room measuring 6 metres by 4 metres. It may be possible to split the room to provide two bedrooms, one measuring 4 metres by 4 metres and the other measuring 4 metres by 2 metres. The ideal way of achieving this partitioning is in a flat where a large existing window can be split by a new dividing wall to give natural light to each of the bedrooms. Depending on the layout of the flat, either a new small lobby will need to be incorporated to give separate doors to each of the two bedrooms, or a new door will need to be made in an existing wall.

No planning permission or building regulation approval is required for this type of alteration, although the terms of the head lease will need to be checked to see whether the consent of the leaseholder is required. In those situations where this type of alteration work is possible, the increase in the value of the flat, particularly if it is in virtually any part of London, greatly exceeds the cost of the work. These particular properties do not come up very often, so when such an opportunity does arise, don't miss it.

Potential for a roof garden

Another attractive possibility that should not be missed is a top-floor flat that has access to the roof, which has the potential to be turned into a roof garden. Nowadays in London it is unlikely that permission will

(continues on page 76)

EXAMPLE 6

Adding value by carrying out a cosmetic modernisation

This example outlines the purchase and letting of a flat in Chelsea, London SW3, with two bedrooms, one bathroom and one shower room. The flat has a 78-year lease, a share of the freehold and car parking. It is in a purpose-built block (1970s) with 24-hour porterage.

The assumptions are that:
- the flat requires modernisation
- buying agents are used at every stage
- flat prices in London SW3 increase by 6.5% pa over five years
- rental incomes in London SW3 increase by 6.5% pa over five years, and
- expenses increase by 6.5% pa over five years.

After five years, the **total pre-tax return** on capital invested is **15.7% pa net** (8.5% pa return on capital plus 7.2% pa return on income), as shown in the table below.

CAPITAL	Value of house after 5 years	Total acquisition costs over 5 years	Net capital gain	Percentage return pa
	£404,175	£283,718	£120,457	8.5%[1]

INCOME	Total rental income over 5 years	Total expenses over 5 years	Net income gain	Percentage return pa
	£102,545	£49,199	£53,346	7.2%[2]

1   £120,457 as a percentage of £283,718 = 42.4%, and 42.4% ÷ 5 = 8.5% pa
2   £102,545 as a percentage of £283,718 = 36.1%, and 36.1% ÷ 5 = 7.2% pa

More detailed analysis

Ⓐ Projection of acquisition costs and net income

Acquisition and refurbishment costs	£
Purchase price	240,000
Acquisition costs: legal fees, stamp duty, valuation fee (an estimated 3.5% + VAT)	9,870
Buying agent's fee (1.5% + VAT)	4,230
Refurbishment costs (including VAT)	22,325
Project management fee for modernisation (12.5% + VAT)	3,279
Part-furnishing package (ie carpets, curtains and white goods only)	3,500
Project management fee for furnishing (12.5% of part-furnishing package + VAT)	514
Total costs	**£283,718**

Valuation on completion of all works = £295,000

Letting income
Let @ £525 per week but allowing 1 month void pa = £25,025 pa
Gross yield = 8.8% pa

Less the following annual maintenance costs:	£
Letting and management fee (15% + VAT)	4,410
Service charge	2,824
Contents insurance	220
Statutory inspections	190
Allowance for general maintenance	350
Tax return work	120
Total expenses	**£8,114**

Total anticipated net income = £16,911 pa
Net yield = 6.0% pa

Ⓑ Projection of return on capital invested

Assuming that both capital and rental values each grow by 6.5% pa over the five-year period, capital and income growth projections are as follows.

Capital growth
This is based on the value on completion of all works of £295,000.

Compound growth at 6.5% on £295,000:
Year 1   295,000 + 19,175 = £314,175
Year 2   314,175 + 20,421 = £334,596
Year 3   334,596 + 21,749 = £356,345
Year 4   356,345 + 23,162 = £379,507
Year 5   379,507 + 24,668 = £404,175

New value after 5 years = £404,175

The total acquisition costs are £283,718. Furnishings are depreciated to nil over five years and the total acquisition costs of £14,100 (legal fees, stamp duty, buying agent's fee etc) are written off in Year 1.

Net capital gain therefore is £404,175 less £283,718 = £120,457. When expressed as an increase on total costs of £283,718, the net capital gain is 42% or, when apportioned over five years, it is 8.5% pa.

Income growth
This is based on the anticipated net income figure of £16,911. It assumes that the annual expenses deducted of £8,114 also increase by 6.5% pa (totalling £49,199 over five years).

Compound growth at 6.5% on £16,911:
Year 1   16,911 + 1,099 = £18,010
Year 2   18,010 + 1,171 = £19,181
Year 3   19,181 + 1,247 = £20,428
Year 4   20,428 + 1,328 = £21,756
Year 5   21,756 + 1,414 = £23,170

Total income over 5 years =   £102,545

So, total acquisition costs are £283,718, while total income over five years is £102,545. This income apportioned over five years gives a figure of £20,509 pa, while income growth is 7.2% pa.

Total return
Therefore, the total return over five years is **8.5% pa capital growth + 7.2% pa income growth**, which gives a **15.7% pa pre-tax return** on capital invested.

be granted for a new floor of accommodation, but adding a roof garden is often an easier option. Planning permission is required to convert a flat roof to a roof garden, but in fact there are thousands of examples in London of existing attractive roof gardens that have been installed without planning permission.

It would cost an average of around £10,000 to make a really attractive roof garden with an automatic watering system. However, the addition to the value of a two-bedroom flat in one of the better parts of London can easily be as much as £30,000.

Upgrading a Victorian house

The Victorian house in Example 7 (see pages 77–79) is more or less an identical property to that in Example 1, Chapter 1 (see pages 23–25). It is in good overall condition but at some stage it has lost many of its original Victorian features. In particular, at some time in the past the original fireplaces were removed or covered over, the panelled doors were boarded over each side and generally the house has been 'modernised' to resemble a 1960s-built house on the inside rather than a house built in the 1890s. These types of house are surprisingly common in many towns and cities in the United Kingdom and offer exceptional opportunities for adding value. This is particularly true if, apart from the devaluing 'modernisation', they have been kept in good overall condition.

The reason why these houses are such an attractive opportunity is because they are not usually advertised as requiring modernisation or upgrading but are simply sold as 'well maintained' terraced houses. This means that the competition to buy them is much less intense because the potential is not so obvious.

Fashions have changed, and in most towns and cities in the United Kingdom the vast majority of purchasers are looking for Victorian (or Edwardian) houses with original features. So demand for these properties is considerably greater than for similar properties without the period features. As a result, these types of house with their original features intact are worth up to 20 per cent more than identical properties that have had the period features removed or covered over.

However, the cost of replacing the missing original features with reclaimed or reproduction items, if they are carefully bought, is much less than the 20 per cent premium. These properties therefore provide the opportunity for an immediate substantial uplift in value for relatively little work. In addition, the process of returning a house to its former glory is particularly satisfying from the investor's point of view.

In general, investors should avoid modernised Victorian or Edwardian houses that have had all the original windows replaced with PVC or other modern windows which are out of keeping with the house. The cost of replacement windows with the correct wooden

(continues on page 80)

EXAMPLE 7

Adding value by upgrading a Victorian house

This example deals with the purchase and letting of a freehold Victorian terraced house in Cambridge, which has three bedrooms and one bathroom.

In this example the assumptions are that:
* the house is in good order, but was modernised in the 1960s
* buying agents are used at every stage
* house prices in Cambridge increase at 5% pa over five years
* rental incomes in Cambridge increase at 5% pa over five years, and
* expenses increase at 5% pa over five years.

After five years, the **total pre-tax return** on capital invested is **14.7% pa net** (6.1% pa on capital plus 8.6% pa on income), as shown in the table below.

CAPITAL	Value of house after 5 years	Total acquisition costs over 5 years	Net capital gain	Percentage return pa
	£134,008	£102,696	£31,312	6.1%[1]

INCOME	Total rental income over 5 years	Total expenses over 5 years	Net income gain	Percentage return pa
	£44,315	£16,319	£27,996	8.6%[2]

1   *£31,312 as a percentage of £102,696 = 30.5%, and 30.5% ÷ 5 = 6.1% pa*
2   *£44,315 as a percentage of £102,696 = 43.2%, and 43.2% ÷ 5 = 8.6% pa*

More detailed analysis

A Projection of acquisition costs and net income

Acquisition and refurbishment costs	£
Purchase price	84,000
Acquisition costs: legal fees, stamp duty, valuation fees (an estimated 3.5% + VAT)	3,454
Acquisition consultant's fee (1.5% + VAT)	1,480
Upgrading cost (including VAT)	8,500
Project management fee for the upgrading (12.5% of upgrading cost + VAT)	1,248
Part-furnishing package (ie carpets, curtains and white goods only)	3,500
Project management fee (12.5% of part furnishing package + VAT)	514
Total costs	**£102,696**

Valuation on completion of all works = £105,000

Letting income
Let @ £950 pcm but allowing 1 month void pa = £10,450 pa
Gross yield = 10.2% pa

Less the following annual maintenance costs:	£
Letting and management fee (15% + VAT)	1,842
Insurance	300
Statutory inspections	150
Garden maintenance	100
Allowance for general maintenance	300
Tax return work	120
Total expenses	**£2,812**

Total anticipated net income = £7,638 pa
Net yield = 7.4% pa

B Projection of return on capital invested

Assuming that capital and rental values each grow by 5% pa over the five-year period, capital and income growth projections are as follows.

Capital growth
This is based on £105,000, the value of the property on completion of the upgrading work (see Example 1), and not the total cost figure of £102,696.

Compound growth at 5% on £105,000:

Year 1	105,000	+ 5,250	=	£110,250
Year 2	110,250	+ 5,512	=	£115,762
Year 3	115,762	+ 5,788	=	£121,550
Year 4	121,550	+ 6,077	=	£127,627
Year 5	127,627	+ 6,381	=	£134,008

New value after 5 years = £134,008

The total acquisition and refurbishment costs are £102,696. After five years, furnishings are depreciated to nil and the total acquisition costs of £4,934 (legal fees, stamp duty, acquisition fee etc) are written off in Year 1.

Net capital gain is therefore £134,008 less £102,696 = £31,312. When expressed as an increase on total costs of £102,696, the net capital gain is 30.5% or, when apportioned over five years, it is 6.1% pa.

Income growth
This is based on the anticipated net income figure of £7,638. It assumes that the annual expenses deducted of £2,812 also increase by 5% pa (totalling £16,319 over five years).

Compound growth at 5% on £7,638:

Year 1	7,638	+ 382	=	£8,020
Year 2	8,020	+ 401	=	£8,421
Year 3	8,421	+ 421	=	£8,842
Year 4	8,842	+ 442	=	£9,284
Year 5	9,284	+ 464	=	£9,748

Total income over 5 years = £44,315

So, total acquisition and refurbishment costs are £102,696, while total income over five years is £44,315. This income apportioned over five years gives a figure of £8,863 pa, while income growth is 8.6% pa.

Total return
Therefore the total return over five years is **6.1% pa capital growth + 8.6% pa income growth**, which gives a **14.7% pa pre-tax return** on capital invested.

frames in the style of the originals is extremely expensive and will reduce the added value profit considerably.

A suitable house is therefore one that has the original sash windows and that generally has been maintained in good order but has had most, if not all, of the period features removed or covered over. The perfect situation is where the period features appear to have been removed but in fact have been simply covered over. It is quite common to find that Victorian and Edwardian houses have had the original fireplaces covered over with asbestos or wooden panels and the original panelled doors have been similarly boarded over.

In Example 7 we have assumed that the original fireplaces and panelled doors have been covered over and that the following work is required:

- to expose and clean all existing Victorian fireplaces, with two fireplaces in particular requiring reclaimed wooden surrounds
- to remove boarding from all existing panelled doors and have all original panelled doors stripped by sending them away to a local pine stripper
- to replace the modern glass front door with a quality panelled front door
- to have a local joiner make up and fit the missing dado rail to the front hall and staircase, and the missing picture rails to both downstairs reception rooms and to all three bedrooms
- to replace the 1960s skirting boards with traditional skirting in all rooms
- to have plaster coving fitted in the entrance hall, front and rear reception rooms and in the main bedroom
- to have simple plaster ceiling roses installed in the front and rear reception rooms, and in the main bedroom
- to have the existing wooden floors sanded and repaired where necessary
- to fit quality brass door furniture throughout the house, but leave light switches and sockets in white plastic
- to install false ceilings with downlights in the kitchen and bathroom
- to replace the kitchen cupboards with reasonable quality units to a total value (including fitting but excluding appliances) of £1,000 (allow £2,500 if the property is in the Greater London area, as tenants tend to expect better quality units). These amounts are quite adequate for average properties to be let. Except for extremely high rental properties, it is a complete waste of money to spend more. If a two-bedroom flat in Earls Court has a £9,000 kitchen instead of a good £2,500 kitchen, it is very unlikely to produce even one pound of extra rental per annum.
- to have the white bathroom suite professionally cleaned (the existing porcelain and cast iron suite is of good quality) and change

the existing ugly modern taps for quality heavy Victorian-style chrome or brass taps; re-tile the bathroom in a quality plain colour such as white, dark blue or dark red and have a dado china rail added at the top of the tiling

- to redecorate the property throughout leaving all panelled doors and floors in their stripped polished state; the kitchen and bathroom should have vinyl floors in plain colours or simple patterns, and
- as with all properties to let, the rear and small front gardens should simply be grassed or, preferably, paved to provide minimum maintenance for tenants.

The above work will transform the appeal of the house and should, assuming the house is in a reasonably good location and was bought at the right price, increase its value by approximately 20 per cent. By careful management of the building work, the total cost for the above work should come to no more than £8,500 including VAT and including £1,000 which has been allowed for miscellaneous repairs in addition to the work specified above. This work would take a maximum of four weeks to complete and would require no building regulation or planning approval assuming that the property is not listed.

The key, as in all refurbishment situations, is for the investor to be absolutely clear in his mind from studying comparable houses in nearby streets what the property will be worth in its finished state and to obtain fixed building quotations for all work required before exchanging contracts on the purchase. This simple but fundamental rule is essential for maximising gains, but it is often ignored by amateur investors. The tightest control of building costs must always be maintained.

In Example 7 it is assumed that buying agents are used throughout the purchase and subsequent work to restore the property's original features. A detailed appraisal with fixed prices should be submitted by the buying agents prior to exchange of contract satisfying the investor on all the above facts. If they are unable to do so then either they have chosen the wrong property or they are the wrong buying agents, or possibly both.

As can be seen from this example, an immediate capital gain is achieved, the value of the property on completion being £105,000 plus the value of the part-furnishing package compared to total costs of £102,696. If buying agents are not used, then the immediate capital gain would be substantially greater. Example 7 assumes that the period fireplaces and panelled doors are hidden but are still in place. If both features have been taken out completely then such items can be acquired from reclamation yards. However, it is only worth installing a reclaimed period fireplace in the sitting-room. False fireplaces would be sufficient in the rear reception room and the main bedroom.

If you decide to install a reclaimed fireplace, be aware that reclamation yards in the north of England have greater availability of stock and lower prices than those in the south. It may pay to buy reclaimed fireplaces from one of the northern yards even if the house that is being upgraded is in the south. The same advice applies to the panelled doors. Reclaimed panelled doors cut to size look far better, particularly when stripped, than purpose-made panelled doors. Purpose-made doors also have the disadvantage of being much more expensive.

If a reclaimed fireplace and panelled doors are necessary, then the potential gain will not be as great as when they already exist but are merely covered. However, the additional cost of buying these items should be no more than £600 for the reclaimed Victorian fireplace and around £40 per reclaimed panelled door.

As in the modernisation of the flat in the Example 6 (see pages 73–75), the added value achieved by upgrading the Victorian house comes in the first year of ownership. Therefore to maximise returns, it would again make sense to sell the property as an up and running investment if another situation with good potential for adding value can be identified.

Settlement or structural problems

A house suffering from a structural defect, particularly settlement, may seem a dangerous opportunity and one to be avoided. Settlement means that the foundations of a property have moved, either downwards or sideways or even, occasionally, upwards. This causes the property that is built on these foundations to move, usually resulting in cracks and sloping floors.

However, for specific types of structural defects the potential for adding value is excellent allowing substantial and immediate capital gains to be achieved. Certainly, though, all houses suffering from settlement or structural problems other than the specific situations outlined in this chapter are strictly to be avoided.

The most commonly encountered and one of the most attractive opportunities is a perfectly good Victorian or Edwardian house (normally terraced) which is, nevertheless, suffering from what may appear to be severe structural problems at the rear of the property. Over a period of years the double storey rear extension with a kitchen on the ground floor and a bathroom above may have subsided to produce internal and external cracking and distorted doorways. Houses put up for sale in such a condition are often executor sales where the ageing owner-occupier was either unaware of the problem, or did not have the finances or motivation to put the problem right. It is quite common for such properties to require additional refurbishment apart from the subsidence at the rear, but for the sake of this illustration it is assumed that the only defect is the settlement at the rear. If other refurbishment is required, that should also be reflected in the asking price giving further potential for adding value. It is important to note, however, that houses with settlement at the side or at the front of the property should be avoided as often the defect is then due to serious ground problems.

The reason why many Victorian and Edwardian houses develop settlement at the rear is because the drains run to the rear of the property and quite commonly have not been replaced since they were installed. Over a period of years the drains start to leak. This softens the ground to the rear of the house so that the foundations and the two floors above start to sink. The effects of this type of defect look serious and make the house, in most circumstances, unmortgageable. When such properties come onto the market they are, almost always, highly discounted in price. A small building firm or developer with the right experience will, however, happily buy such properties and make substantial profits.

The defect appears severe but is in fact simply remedied. To replace a short run of drain at the rear and, as is typical, to underpin about half the footings of the rear extension should cost no more than £8,000 including VAT. This figure includes the cost of straightening the internal doors, levelling the two internal floors and filling cracks. Typically this work would take no more than two to three weeks, and would immediately make the house mortgageable and reinsurable as regards subsidence. The resulting jump in value would be around 25 per cent to 30 per cent.

In order to ascertain whether the settlement is only due to a leaking drain, do not have a full structural survey carried out by a chartered surveyor. Instead go directly to a local firm of consulting engineers and agree an hourly rate to inspect and report on the problem. Instructing a full structural survey will cost a considerable amount of money and almost inevitably the chartered surveyor will only recommend that a specialist report is obtained from a structural engineer. By going straight to a structural engineer, a simple report that pinpoints the problem can be obtained immediately and often it will cost less than £100. A good local engineer will also recommend several builders experienced in underpinning work and arrange for quotations to be submitted. It is important to remember that the underpinning work will have to be supervised by a structural engineer and will require building regulation approval.

Local council grants for this type of work are available, in some circumstances, to investor landlords. At the time of publication of this book, all local authorities still provide grants to landlords to improve properties that are then let out. The existence of landlords' grants are not well known and the bureaucracy involved in obtaining one is considerable. However, there is no means test and the basic requirements are that the property must not be sold for a minimum of five years (otherwise a proportion of the grant is repayable), and that the property must be let as a single occupancy and not as a multiple occupancy.

The formula used by local councils to decide on the amount of grant to award is based on the increase in rental values. Although complex, having mastered the workings of the formula it is comparatively easy to identify which properties are likely to obtain the highest grants. Currently the maximum landlords' grant that is available to refurbish a property to let out is £25,000. A good acquisition consultant will advise as to the availability of such grants and will often charge a proportion of the grant awarded as a fee for obtaining it. Alternatively, the housing officer from the local council will provide guidance notes and should be prepared to spend some time explaining the workings of the system.

The property in Example 8 (see pages 85–87) is more or less identical to the property in Example 1, Chapter 1 (see pages 23–25) – a freehold Victorian terraced house in Cambridge – except that it has settlement to the rear of the house caused by a leaking drain. Once the remedial work has been carried out, the property is worth £105,000 – the same as the property in Example 1. However, total costs in Example 1 are £115,183 whereas in Example 8 they are just £87,302, representing a substantial capital gain.

As in the other examples in this chapter, the added value in Example 8 comes at the start of ownership and capital growth for the five-year period is only the average 5 per cent per annum. Therefore it would be sensible to sell the property as an up and running investment in the first year.

Remedial work on non-regulation brickwork

Another quite common structural problem that is simple to remedy and provides scope for considerable added value is a house, usually Victorian, that has one or more external walls built of 4.5-inch brickwork instead of 9-inch brickwork. Such brickwork was surprisingly common when Victorian builders sought to maximise profits at a time when building regulations were considerably less strict than they are today. Some of the most profitable purchases to be found are Victorian houses that have the side external wall into which the chimney stack is built constructed of 4.5-inch brickwork and that may also have a single-storey rear extension constructed of 4.5-inch brickwork.

As in the leaking drain example earlier, such circumstances result in the house often being unmortgageable and being offered for sale at a heavily discounted price. Again, the answer is to instruct a good local consulting engineer to advise. In the situation where the side wall of the house that has been built of 4.5-inch brickwork is the wall into

(continues on page 88)

EXAMPLE 8

Adding value by rectifying subsidence to the rear of a house

This example deals with the purchase and letting of a freehold Victorian terraced house in Cambridge, which has three bedrooms and one bathroom.

In this example the assumptions are that:
- the house is in good order throughout apart from structural problems at the rear, which are ascertained to be caused by a leaking drain
- buying agents are used at every stage
- house prices in Cambridge increase at 5% pa over five years
- rental incomes in Cambridge increase at 5% pa over five years, and
- expenses increase at 5% pa over five years.

After five years, the **total pre-tax return** on capital invested is **20.9% pa net** (10.7% pa on capital plus 10.2% pa on income), as shown in the table below.

CAPITAL	Value of house after 5 years	Total acquisition costs over 5 years	Net capital gain	Percentage return pa
	£134,008	£87,302	£46,706	10.7%[1]

INCOME	Total rental income over 5 years	Total expenses over 5 years	Net income gain	Percentage return pa
	£44,315	£16,319	£27,996	10.2%[2]

1   *£46,706 as a percentage of £87,302 = 53.5%, and 53.5% ÷ 5 = 10.7% pa*
2   *£44,315 as a percentage of £87,302 = 50.8%, and 50.8% ÷ 5 = 10.2% pa*

More detailed analysis

Ⓐ Projection of acquisition costs and net income

Acquisition and refurbishment costs	£
Purchase price	70,000
Acquisition costs: legal fees, stamp duty, valuation fees (an estimated 3.5% + VAT)	2,879
Acquisition consultant's fee (1.5% + VAT)	1,234
Remedial work (including VAT)	8,000
Project management fee for remedial work (12.5% + VAT)	1,175
Part-furnishing package (ie carpets, curtains and white goods only)	3,500
Project management fee for furnishing (12.5% of part furnishing package + VAT)	514
Total costs	**£87,302**

Letting income
Let @ £950 pcm but allowing 1 month void pa = £10,450 pa
Gross yield = 12% pa

Less the following annual maintenance costs:	£
Letting and management fee (15% + VAT)	1,842
Insurance	300
Statutory inspections	150
Garden maintenance	100
Allowance for general maintenance	300
Tax return work	120
Total expenses	**£2,812**

Total anticipated net income = £7,638 pa
Net yield = 8.7% pa

Ⓑ Projection of return on capital invested

Assuming that capital and rental values each grow by 5% pa over the five-year period, capital and income growth projections are as follows.

Capital growth
This is based on £105,000, the value of the house when repaired (see Example 1) and not the total cost figure of £87,302.

Compound growth at 5% on £105,000:

Year 1	105,000	+	5,250	=	£110,250
Year 2	110,250	+	5,512	=	£115,762
Year 3	115,762	+	5,788	=	£121,550
Year 4	121,550	+	6,077	=	£127,627
Year 5	127,627	+	6,381	=	£134,008

New value after 5 years = £134,008

The total acquisition and refurbishment costs are £87,302. After five years, furnishings are depreciated to nil and the total acquisition costs of £4,113 (legal fees, stamp duty, acquisition fee etc) are written off in Year 1.

Net capital gain is therefore £134,008 less £87,302 = £46,706. When expressed as an increase on total costs of £87,302, the net capital gain is 53.5% or, when apportioned over five years, it is 10.7% pa.

Income growth
This is based on the anticipated net income figure of £7,638. It assumes that the annual expenses deducted of £2,812 also increase by 5% pa (totalling £16,319 over five years).

Compound growth at 5% on £7,638:

Year 1	7,638	+	382	=	£8,020
Year 2	8,020	+	401	=	£8,421
Year 3	8,421	+	421	=	£8,842
Year 4	8,842	+	442	=	£9,284
Year 5	9,284	+	464	=	£9,748

Total income over 5 years   £44,315

So, total acquisition and refurbishment costs are £87,302, while total income over five years is £44,315. This income apportioned over five years gives a figure of £8,863 pa, while income growth is 10.2% pa.

Total return
Therefore the total return over five years is **10.7% pa capital growth + 10.2% pa income growth**, which gives a **20.9% pa pre-tax return** on capital invested.

which the chimney is built, almost certainly the engineer will confirm that all that is required is studwork plasterboard with appropriate insulation on the inside of the wall either side of the fireplace, both upstairs and downstairs. This is a very straightforward job, which typically costs less than a £1,000. Similarly with the single-storey rear extension, the consulting engineer is likely to advise that all that is required is the same treatment.

The situations to avoid are:
● where the rear extension is built of 4.5-inch brickwork and is built on two storeys, or
● where the side wall built of 4.5-inch brickwork is the side of the house without the chimney.

In both these circumstances the houses should be avoided and money should not be wasted on a consultant engineer's report as expensive remedial work will be required.

Fire-damaged properties

Another renovation possibility, although they only come up for sale occasionally, are lightly fire-damaged houses. Quite often these offer astonishing value for money and wide scope for adding value. Typically these are houses that have suffered a kitchen fire and the whole house has been smoke damaged. Internally the houses look appalling, but in fact they often only require professional cleaning and redecorating.

Properties with scope for an extra bedroom in the roof space

For this opportunity to add value, particular attention must be paid to the location and value of the property. While the cost of providing a bedroom in the roof space will be the same regardless of the town or city in which the house is located, the added value of a third bedroom will vary dramatically. In a poor location, providing a bedroom in the roof space may not add any more value than the cost of installing the bedroom, and in some locations it can actually be less.

Therefore to maximise the gain on this type of work, properties with unconverted roof spaces should be sought in the best locations. In a city such as Cambridge, a well converted bedroom with an *en suite* shower in a good street will add £25,000–£30,000 to the value, with the conversion itself costing less than £10,000. A good terraced house in Fulham, London SW6, would increase in value by £40,000–£50,000 by the addition of a third bedroom and bathroom in the roof space, while the total conversion costs should be no more than around £15,000.

Looking at a potential conversion from a financial point of view, the existing roof space must be big enough to accommodate a new bedroom without lowering the floor or raising the roof. Any competent builder will advise whether the existing roof space is large enough to convert from a practical point of view and to comply with building regulations. It is often the case that specialist loft conversion companies are unnecessarily expensive and tend to over-design, so it is better to use a small competent general builder or, best of all, act as the main contractor yourself. When it comes to adding value the golden rule is to keep building costs to a minimum.

The advantage of this opportunity for adding value is that suitable properties are still comparatively numerous and no planning permission is required as long as the property is neither a listed building nor in a conservation area. To avoid the need for planning permission, it is necessary that light to the new bedroom is provided by way of Velux windows to the rear of the property. The insertion of dormer windows will require planning permission (and will not necessarily add to the value) and, although it is a slightly grey area, it is safest to assume that planning permission is also required for Velux windows to the front of the property. Building regulation approval is certainly required for loft conversions, but this is a straightforward procedure that is handled by your buying agent or, in the case of a buying agent not being used, then by your builder.

An important point to bear in mind is that if a three-storey property is to be let under multiple occupancy (for example, four or five individuals, other than from the same family, such as students), then building regulations will require expensive additional work (a protected staircase, emergency lighting, etc) for fire safety reasons. Therefore to maximise on the return, properties that are to be let following conversion of the roof space (making it a three-storey building) should be let to one family in order to avoid the costly and unsightly additional works that would be required if letting the property as a shared house.

As always with adding value, the key is to do your homework fully and competently before making the purchase. How much will an additional bedroom with or without an *en suite* shower or bathroom add to the value of the property being considered given its particular location? How much can the property be bought for and exactly what would the cost of the conversion work be? When the figures all add up to a worthwhile increase in value over costs, then proceed. When they don't add up favourably, reject the opportunity and look at another one.

Properties with scope for an extension to the rear

No planning permission is required to extend a property with a single-storey extension to the rear provided that the following three circumstances apply.

1. The total area of the extension does not exceed more than 10 per cent of the existing floor area of the house. This is called a permitted development right (PDR) and applies to all houses other than those where PDRs have been excluded in the original planning permission or where the PDRs have already been utilised by such an extension. Conversion of the loft space is permitted under PDRs, but it does not count as part of the 10 per cent as it is existing space, not new space.

2. The ground taken up by the new rear extension does not exceed 50 per cent of the total area of the rear garden.

3. The property must not be listed or in a conservation area.

In addition, the owner's solicitor needs to check that there isn't a valid restrictive covenant that affects rights to extend the property.

If all these factors apply, an existing three-bedroom house totalling 120 square metres in total could have an extension to the rear of the property of up to 12 square metres without the need for planning consent.

Building regulations would be required for such an extension, but this is a straightforward and simple matter which the builder carrying out the work would advise on. Even though the extension is new, VAT would be chargeable on the works and would not be recoverable by the investor.

The amount spent on the extension should be kept to a minimum. An architect is not necessary or desirable for such an extension. It is better to have some simple plans drawn up by a draughtsman who has been recommended by local estate agents or by the builder. The real cost in building an extension is the provision of services – central heating, bathrooms and kitchens.

A rear extension of 12 square metres, which gives a fairly large room of 4 metres by 3 metres, would be designed with features such as french windows facing onto the garden, an electric heater with a thermostat and, if there is room, a pitched roof, but otherwise a flat roof. Such an extension should cost no more than £550 per square metre (a total cost of £6,600 + VAT = £7,755), but depending on the location of the property the increase in value could easily be double that amount.

The use of the room either as a third reception room or a fourth/fifth bedroom will depend on the requirements of the tenants. If such a property is let as a shared house, then taking an average rental of £50 per week for the value of the room as an extra bedroom gives an additional gross rental income of £2,600 per annum (£2,383 when allowing one month void). This gross rental income expressed as a percentage of the capital cost of £7,050 gives a gross return on the additional capital employed of 37 per cent per annum.

Properties with potential for an additional housing plot

Properties with the potential to create an additional plot for another house either to the side or the rear arise infrequently, but they do come up. Even amateur investors occasionally find themselves in the fortunate position of having bought a house with development potential in the garden. Many vendors are not aware of the value that part of their garden has for development purposes. Such owners are totally at the mercy of the selling estate agent. Only if the agent points out to the vendor that planning permission should be applied for on part of the garden is the vendor made aware of the potential to add significant value. Many estate agents do, of course, point this out to the vendor, but on some occasions they fail to do so, either from lack of experience or lack of attention to the property being sold.

The most obvious situation is where an end of terrace property is being bought that has a garden to the side as well as to the rear providing enough space to build another terraced house to the side. The person with whom to discuss this possibility is certainly not the selling estate agent. Instead, the most direct approach is to speak to the local planning officer who will give an informal opinion as to whether planning permission would be forthcoming.

Planning officers vary enormously around the country in their degree of helpfulness but all, if pressed, will give an informal indication. They will always emphasise that the final decision to grant planning permission is not made by the planning officers but by committee members. In practice, however, in the majority of cases the committee members will follow the planning officers' recommendations. Therefore, if a planning officer suggests informally that they will support an application for an additional house to the side of an existing house, then it is reasonable to believe that such planning permission will be forthcoming.

Although the percentage varies from one part of the country to another, a reasonable estimate is that a plot of land with planning permission to build a new house is worth around 35 per cent of the end value of the house (much more in London and expensive locations). Therefore, if it is determined that the end-of-terrace house to be built would have a value on completion of £100,000, then the value of the plot with planning permission would be around £35,000. In virtually all areas of the United Kingdom there is a ready demand from builders, developers and private individuals to buy plots of land with planning permission and therefore they are extremely saleable.

Similarly, opportunities do arise to obtain planning permission to build a new detached house at the rear of a property with a long garden. These situations are most common where the house being bought has a corner plot with a long rear garden running down the street to the side. The bottom half of such a rear garden may well have the potential to build a new house fronting the side street, again creating an immediate substantial capital gain.

Buying a building plot and constructing a new house on it

Often ignored by amateur investors, the new build option can provide exceptional returns. The process is relatively straightforward and, provided the right procedures are followed, excellent returns are virtually guaranteed. One difficulty, however, is the shortage of individual plots with planning permission in good letting locations. They do exist in all towns and cities, and although patience and determination are required, opportunities will arise on a regular basis.

The rationale behind buying a building plot is simple. If a brand new property is bought from a house builder for £100,000, then it is a safe assumption that around 15 per cent of that £100,000 is the house builder's profit. So only £85,000 has actually been paid for the land and the house constructed on it. By buying the land and constructing the house, an investor becomes the house builder and saves the £15,000 that he would have paid over to the house builder.

To identify the right site, it is essential to register an interest in building plots with every estate agent in the town that is being targeted and to telephone all of them at least once every week to see if they have anything coming up. Emphasise that you are in a position to exchange contracts extremely quickly.

Another option that works well is to place an advertisement in the local newspaper stating that you are looking for a building plot with planning permission in a particular area. Some vendors do not like using estate agents and prefer to deal with purchasers direct, and so such advertisements often get results.

Another good source of information about potential building plots is local architects. Also, ask the local authority to send you copies of all new planning applications made each month. Most councils charge a small fee for this, but it is useful for identifying plots that have just received planning permission. The new application information sent out by the local council always includes the owner's or the estate agent's name and address, and this makes it easy to approach them direct to see if they wish to sell.

The New Build Examples 1 and 2 (see pages 94–95 and 96–97) illustrate the difference between an investor developing a house himself as opposed to buying the house from a developer. Example 1 assumes that buying agents are used throughout, while Example 2 assumes the investor is handling the project himself.

There are a small number of buying agents that specialise in identifying new build opportunities for clients and then managing the whole project. Unless the investor lives locally, the new build option should only be considered if full professional advice is taken throughout the project. However, if you live near to the building plot and are prepared to devote the necessary time to the project, there is absolutely no reason why a new build cannot be undertaken by an investor without using a buying agent. Key factors of 'going it alone' are as follows.

1. It is essential prior to exchange of contracts to check that the planning permission contains no onerous or unusual conditions.

2. If the site has outline planning consent as opposed to detailed consent, careful checks must be made with the local planning authority as to exactly what size and design of house will be permitted.

3. It is essential to obtain a soil test report prior to exchange of contracts to ensure that there are no unusual ground conditions.

4. It is essential to use a National House Building Council (NHBC) registered house builder and to obtain at least three quotations for the building works.

5. An architect will be required to prepare working drawings, building regulation approval and to monitor construction. The architect will also be able to arrange for soil tests to be carried out prior to exchange of contracts and for those soil tests to be checked by a structural engineer to confirm that there are no unusual ground conditions.

6. A formal building contract should be entered into with the builder providing not only for a fixed price but for penalties in the event of the house not being finished by an agreed date. The architect will advise on the form of this building contract.

7. The architect will check (prior to exchange of contracts) that all services are available and that the cost of connecting to the services (ie water, drainage and electricity) will be included within the house builder's price.

It may all sound a rather daunting process, but in fact it is not. In many ways, building a new house is far simpler and more straightforward than a major refurbishment, and the rewards are often greater. As in all cases, when researching a proposition the important thing is to do all the figures prior to commitment. Make sure you research the answers to all these questions.

● What is the site going to cost?
● What will professional fees add up to?
● Which is the best fixed price contract building contract you have received to build the property?
● How long will it take to build the property and what do the interest charges add up to? (If using cash, then money should be costed out at the same return that you would have received from a building society deposit.)

(continues on page 98)

NEW BUILD EXAMPLE 1

Using a buying agent

Acquisition and build costs	£
Purchase of plot with planning permission	40,000
Acquisition costs: legal fees, etc including fixed fee of £1,500 + VAT to buying agent	2,600
Build costs @ £550 per square metre for an approximate 100 square metre build area	55,000
Project management fee to buying agent (12.5% of build costs + VAT)	8,078
Professional fees: preparation of working drawings by architect, soil test reports, calculations by structural engineer, building regulation fees etc (estimate)	2,400
Part-furnishing package (ie carpets, curtains and white goods only)	3,500
Project management fee for part-furnishing package (12.5% + VAT)	514
Interest charges on land and costs during construction (estimate)	2,460
Total costs	**£114,552**

Valuation on completion = £125,000

Letting income
Let @ £1,000 pcm but allowing 1 month void pa = £11,000 pa
Gross yield = 9.6%

Less the following annual maintenance costs:	£
Letting and management fee (15% + VAT)	1,939
Insurance	300
Statutory inspections	150
Allowance for general maintenance	300
Tax return work	120
Total expenses	**£2,809**

Total anticipated net income = £8,191 pa
Net yield = 7.2%

The investor makes an immediate capital gain of £125,000 on completion (ignoring furnishings) less total costs of £114,552 = £10,448, plus the value of the furnishings.

COMPARED TO:

Identical new property acquired from a builder/developer   £
Purchase price   125,000
Acquisition costs (4.5% + VAT)   6,609
Part-furnishing package   3,500
Project management fee for part-furnishing package
(12.5% + VAT)   514
Total costs   **£135,623**

Letting income
As on page 94 to produce net income of £8,191 pa
Net yield = 6.1%

**The investor makes no immediate capital gain, and in fact
the property needs to increase in value from £125,000 to
£135,623 just to cover acquisition and furnishing expenses.**

NEW BUILD EXAMPLE 2

Not using a buying agent

Acquisition and build costs	£
Purchase of plot with planning permission	40,000
Acquisition costs	850
Build costs @ £550 per square metre for an approximate 100 square metre build area	55,000
Professional fees: architect supervision, preparation of working drawings by architect, soil test reports, calculations by structural engineer, building regulation fees etc (estimate)	3,500
Part-furnishing package (ie carpets, curtains and white goods only)	3,500
Interest charges on land and costs during construction (estimate)	2,460
Total costs	**£105,310**

Valuation on completion = £125,000

Letting income
Let @ £1,000 pcm but allowing 1 month void pa = £11,000 pa
Gross yield = 10.4%

Less the following annual maintenance costs:	£
Letting and management fee (15% + VAT)	1,939
Insurance	300
Statutory inspections	150
Allowance for general maintenance	300
Tax return work	120
Total expenses	**£2,809**

Total anticipated net income = £8,191 pa
Net yield = 7.8%

The investor makes an immediate capital gain of £125,000 on completion (ignoring furnishings) less total costs of £105,310 = £19,690, plus the value of the furnishings.

COMPARED TO:

Identical new property acquired from a builder/developer £
Purchase price   125,000
Acquisition costs (3% + VAT)   4,406
Part-furnishing package   3,500
Total costs   **£132,906**

Letting income
As on page 96 to produce net income of £8,191 pa
Net yield = 6.2%

**The investor makes no immediate capital gain, and in fact
the property needs to increase in value from £125,000 to
£135,109 just to cover acquisition and furnishing expenses.**

● How much will that property be worth on completion? (Obtain at least three estimates of valuation from local estate agents.)

When you know the answers to these questions and you are still happy that the project is worthwhile, then proceed to exchange of contracts. Building a new house is a particularly rewarding experience, and as long as the right checks are carried out and the right builder is chosen carefully, there is no reason why it cannot be an extremely profitable route for the investor.

As can be seen from this chapter, there are a number of ways in which properties being acquired for investment purposes can, by adding value, have an immediate and substantial uplift in capital value with corresponding high rental returns on total costs employed. The best situations, and the ones you are most likely to come across, have been outlined. In practice, many properties offer a combination of the options to add value which can enhance returns even further.

SUMMARY

◆ Adding value is the method of maximising returns from investment in residential property. Only one in many properties inspected will have real prospects for adding value, but when a suitable property is identified the rewards are considerable.

◆ Good buying agents will identify added value situations for clients who specifically request them. If you decide not to use a buying agent, it is essential to be on the spot to control and supervise the entire process.

◆ The formula for adding value is:

'Increase in Value' minus 'Costs of works' = 'Added Value'

Be ruthless in determining whether all costs incurred are actually increasing value and beware of overdesigning and overspending. First-time investors and developers frequently spend too much on renovations and also make improvements that do not add value.

◆ The residential market is both huge and unsophisticated. Whatever the state of the market, there are always opportunities to substantially outperform the residential market as a whole. Becoming an expert on residential property is not difficult provided you have time, enthusiasm and determination. Otherwise, use a buying agent.

CHAPTER 4

Borrowing and gearing

Most people borrow money, usually in the form of a mortgage, when buying their own house to live in. The reason for borrowing this money is, in the majority of cases, because the purchaser has insufficient cash resources to buy his chosen property. Alternatively though, it may be because he wishes to use part of his own capital for purposes other than buying the house in which he lives.

When buying a property for investment purposes, there is good reason to borrow. Borrowing allows the investor to maximise on capital gains in relation to the amount of money invested. Most people are aware that commodity dealers, when buying metals and other such commodities, only provide a small deposit when they make a deal. As a result, even a slight increase in the value of the commodity creates a large gain in relation to the original deposit. Conversely, if the price drops slightly, there is a substantial loss in relation to the deposit made. It is this that makes investment in commodities such a high risk activity.

However, the potential for loss when investing in residential property is much lower than when investing in commodities, especially if the whole project is carefully researched. In fact it makes sound financial sense to maximise capital returns by borrowing, and in business circles borrowing for this reason is usually referred to as 'gearing'.

Gearing

'Gearing', 'leverage' and 'equity to debt ratio' all mean the same thing: borrowing money to increase the return on a fixed amount of capital employed.

For example, if a £100,000 property is bought for cash and increases in value over one year by £5,000, then the return on the capital employed is 5 per cent. If, however, the same property is bought with an 80 per cent mortgage of £80,000, then the capital employed is only £20,000. The gain of £5,000 – 5 per cent of the value of the property – represents a return on the capital employed of 25 per cent instead of just 5 per cent.

If, therefore, instead of buying one property for £100,000 cash, the investor buys four properties, each with a mortgage of £80,000, then in the example on the previous page his capital gain would be £20,000 instead of just £5,000 on the one property. As long as the net income yield of the properties at least equals the average interest rate on the borrowed money, then the income position is unaltered. If the cost of the borrowed money is actually less than the net income yield, then the income position is also increased by gearing up. It is also worth remembering, however, that just as gains are increased by gearing, so are losses in the event of a fall in values.

This explains the basic principles of gearing. Example 9 (see pages 103–105) illustrates the workings of these principles in practice. In this example the mortgage is calculated on the purchase price of the property (ie 80 per cent of £135,000 = £108,000). The total outlay required is the £27,000 balance for the purchase of the property plus £17,700 to cover acquisition costs and furnishings.

As we saw in Chapter 3, when a property is purchased with the potential to add value, the valuation on completion of the project may equal or exceed total costs. In these cases the effect of gearing is even more beneficial than in Example 9.

Remember, though, that for interest payments on the mortgage to be tax deductible the loan must be taken out for the purchase of an investment property. In addition, that loan must be taken out at the same time as buying the property or immediately afterwards. (For further details, see Chapter 7.)

Finance

A mortgage is simply a loan of capital. It is finance from a lending institution borrowed in order to assist with the purchase of a property. The loan itself is secured against the property and typically the borrower is required to make monthly payments to the lender for the use of the money.

Fundamentally, there are two types of mortgage: the repayment (or capital and interest) mortgage, and the interest only mortgage. These are examined in more detail below, along with variable and fixed interest rate mortgages.

Repayment mortgages

The repayment mortgage allows the borrower to repay the money lent by the mortgage provider by making monthly payments of both capital and interest. This means that the loan decreases over the term of the mortgage, eventually reducing to zero and thus ultimately providing the borrower with an unencumbered property. It is probably the most popular type of mortgage for individuals acquiring single or small portfolios of property for investment.

(continues on page 106)

EXAMPLE 9

The purchase of a house in a prime location with an 80 per cent mortgage

This example deals with the purchase and letting of a modern town house with three bedrooms and one bathroom in a prime location.

In this example the assumptions are that:
- the house has been professionally and fully renovated prior to purchase
- a buying agent is used throughout
- house prices increase at 5% pa.

After one year, the **total pre-tax return** on personal capital invested is **15.4% pa net**. This pre-tax return is calculated from the following.

	£		£
Purchase price & acquisition costs	152,700	Capital growth at 5%	6,750
Less 80% mortgage	108,000	Net income after mortgage repayments	129
Capital invested	**£44,700**	**Total return**	**£6,879**

More detailed analysis

Ⓐ Projection of acquisition costs and net income

Acquisition and furnishing costs	£
Purchase price	135,000
Acquisition costs: legal fees, stamp duty, valuation fees (an estimated 3.5% + VAT)	5,552
Buying agent's fee (1.5% + VAT)	2,379
Mortgage sourcing fee (1% of mortgage + VAT)	1,269
Full furnishing package (ie carpets, curtains, furniture, white goods and appliances)	8,500
Total costs	**£152,700**
Less the 80% mortgage	108,000
Total capital required	**£44,700**

Letting income
Let @ £1,300 pcm but allowing 1 month void pa = £14,300 pa
Gross yield = 9.4% pa

Less the following annual maintenance costs:	£
Letting and management fee (15% plus VAT)	2,472
Insurance	300
Statutory inspections	150
Garden maintenance	100
Allowance for general maintenance	300
Tax return work	120
Total expenses	**£3,442**

Total anticipated net income = £10,858 pa
Net yield = 7.1% pa

Mortgage repayments
Annual mortgage repayments (interest only) on the total mortgage of £108,000 over 25 years @ 7.5% pa including full life cover for a male aged 40   £10,729

Hence, the net income from the property fully covers all mortgage repayments. The net income surplus after mortgage repayments are deducted is   £129

Effect of adding capital growth to return on capital
Capital growth of 5% on purchase price of £135,000   £6,750

Total return
(capital growth plus net income surplus)   **£6,879**

Therefore, the **net yield** on the required amount of capital invested
(£6,879 as a percentage of £44,700) is **15.4% pa**.

Most lenders set up a repayment mortgage in such a way that the reduction of capital owed is relatively small throughout much of the mortgage term and only in the latter years does the debt decrease radically. This means that the borrower is virtually paying only interest for the early years of the loan and as the debt moves towards its expiry date, a much higher proportion of the monthly payment is used to repay the capital. If the loan is repaid after only a few years, for example by the sale of the property, then maximum cash flow benefits will have been enjoyed as only interest payments will have been made.

In the case of many repayment mortgages, there is no penalty or other fee for paying off the mortgage early. Therefore it makes sense to take out a repayment mortgage for the maximum number of years, say 20 or 25 years, even if the intention is to repay the mortgage by sale of the property within five years. The longer the original mortgage term, the lower the monthly repayments, and the more cash flow positive the property will be. Alternatively, the borrower has the option of continuing the mortgage for a longer period of time in order to reduce or ultimately pay off the capital outstanding.

Life cover is now only required by a few of the large clearing banks. Virtually all smaller banks and building societies are not concerned that life cover is taken out in connection with a repayment mortgage for investment purposes.

Interest only mortgage
An interest only mortgage is a facility that quite simply requires the repayment of interest to the lender throughout the term. The capital does not reduce over the term of the loan so that when the mortgage term does end the borrower has to repay the capital from his own resources or from the sale of the property itself. This type of mortgage is sometimes backed by some type of investment vehicle to allow the build up of capital in order to repay the money borrowed. Typically an endowment, pension or savings policy is taken out through an insurance company and linked to the mortgage.

This type of limited mortgage is common for owner-occupiers, but is not so popular with investor purchasers. The reasons for this are quite straightforward:
● historically endowment-backed mortgages have shown an extremely poor investment performance, and
● the concept of using one investment vehicle to repay capital on a second investment vehicle can be regarded as an over-complication of the transaction.

Increasingly, lenders no longer require endowment or even life policies for an interest only mortgage. In these instances the only real difference between a repayment mortgage and an interest only mortgage is that with a repayment mortgage there is the discipline of making automatic repayments of capital whereas with the interest only mortgage it is up to the borrower to decide when to make any capital repayments, if at all. So the repayment mortgage provides the discipline of automatic repayments of capital while the interest only mortgage, assuming no endowment policy is required, gives the borrower complete control over capital and repayments.

Therefore, if a decision is made to take out an interest only mortgage, the first thing to check is that the lender does not require an endowment policy. The question of whether the investor requires an endowment, pension or personal equity plan should always be regarded as a totally separate investment issue to the investment in the property itself.

Variable interest rate mortgages

If the borrower takes out a variable rate mortgage, his mortgage repayments will vary in accordance with the mortgage rate set from time to time by the lender. At its most basic level, an increase in interest rates during one month will result in an increase in mortgage payments the following month. Equally, if interest rates go down, so the mortgage payments will decrease the following month. However, many lenders adopt a level payment which is set each year and revised annually to take into account changes in interest rates during the previous year. This is simpler for the borrower and may result in a saving when interest rates are increasing.

Lenders may offer a discount off their variable rate in the first year, or first few years, of the loan itself, after which time it reverts back to the variable rate. This type of mortgage is attractive to investors who intend to sell within the first few years of ownership.

With capped rate mortgages, the interest rate paid by the borrower will not exceed a predetermined level during the term of the cap. This type of product is attractive for investment mortgages as it provides security against large fluctuations in interest rates. There is also the cap and collar mortgage. This type of mortgage protects the lender as well as the borrower because although interest rates are capped for a certain period of time at a maximum interest rate, they are also collared at a minimum interest rate for the same duration.

Another type of mortgage is the deferred interest scheme. A deferred interest mortgage quite simply means that while the standard rate of interest is payable, it is not all payable in the first few years of the mortgage. Payment of some of the interest is deferred to after a fixed period of time. In periods of high interest rates and rapidly rising house prices, deferred schemes are commonly used for owner-occupiers, particularly first-time buyers on restricted incomes.

Some lenders do, from time to time, make them available for investment mortgages and they are attractive products if it is intended to sell the property within a relatively short period of time. However, it is important to examine carefully any penalty payments required for repaying the mortgage within the deferred interest rate period or within a set time after the end of the deferred interest period. Sometimes, even with such penalties, these mortgage deals can still be attractive from a cash flow point of view.

Fixed interest rate mortgages

The most common type of mortgage product available is the fixed rate mortgage. This product ensures that the interest rate remains the same during a predetermined period however much the standard variable rate changes. This type of mortgage is popular with investment borrowers as it means that the borrower knows exactly what the mortgage payments will be for a fixed number of years. At the end of the fixed rate period, the interest rate will revert to the current variable rate, but most lenders will then offer the option to obtain a new fixed rate.

Fixed rate mortgages almost always include penalties for early redemption. For example, a five-year fixed rate mortgage may have a penalty or 'lock-in' period of up to a further five years. The penalty for early redemption may be as much as six or twelve months' interest. What this means is that if the borrower decides to sell the property within the fixed interest period or within the further lock-in period, there is likely to be a substantial penalty payment. So, fixed interest rate mortgages are attractive to medium-term investors, but are unattractive to investors who may wish to realise gains quickly and reinvest their capital elsewhere.

Finding the best deal

The above are the basic mortgage types, but it is important to remember that new products are constantly evolving. Over the next few years the range and types of mortgage available for investment property will substantially increase.

How does the investor go about finding the best investment mortgage deal available? Basically there are two choices:
● source your own mortgage by approaching your bank or a selection of banks and building societies that are advertising the availability of mortgages for investment purposes, or
● instruct a specialised mortgage broker.

Whichever type of mortgage you choose, obtain an 'in principle' mortgage offer before make an offer on a property. To secure the best property opportunities you must be able to move swiftly to exchange of contracts, and that means having the finance in place before you make an offer.

Sourcing your own mortgage

The only advantage to sourcing your own mortgage is that you will not have to pay an arrangement fee to a mortgage broker, although many lenders will still charge an administration fee for setting up and processing the mortgage. Negotiating and sourcing the best investment mortgage product is a time-consuming and specialised business and, with two exceptions, it will almost always pay to approach one of the specialised mortgage brokers.

The first exception is if you approach your own bank. The deal that it offers will, of course, depend on the relationship that you enjoy with it and on its lending policy at the current time. It is a quick and reliable way of testing the market and, if nothing else, will provide you with a standard by which to judge other mortgage offers. In those cases where your own principal residence is not mortgaged, or only has a small mortgage in relation to its value, your own bank is likely to offer some of the most competitive terms to buy one or more investment properties.

The second exception is if you approach your main local building society. Many of the remaining local building societies still provide investment mortgages on properties within their geographical area and, quite often, these mortgages are available at attractive rates.

The problem with approaching the literally hundreds of banks, building societies and other lenders operating within the market is that the time involved in sourcing the best mortgage can be considerable indeed. Almost all lending institutions are somewhat bureaucratic and dealing with them is often a frustrating and exhausting process. Even when you have found a lender who makes an attractive 'in principle' offer to you, you may find that at the eleventh hour, just before exchange of contracts, the building society does not, for example, lend on flats that are situated over commercial premises. Unfortunately banks and building societies do not always make a point of making all their rules and regulations regarding lending criteria known at the outset, and often these matters emerge only following a survey and valuation.

Selecting the right mortgage broker

It is extraordinarily easy to set up in business as a mortgage broker and the Sunday newspapers are full of advertisements placed by mortgage brokers providing so-called 'specialised services'. In reality, many of these brokers are no more than one-man bands, often with quite limited experience.

Arranging investment mortgages, particularly for expatriates and foreign nationals, is a highly specialised business and the average mortgage broker is unlikely to be able to source the best deals or obtain offers quickly. Some, but by no means all, buying agents have their own in-house mortgage brokerage service. At the end of this book (see Useful Addresses) there is a selection of mortgage brokers who do specialise in arranging investment mortgages and can be relied on to source the best mortgage deal for you and to explain the precise terms of the mortgage offered in a clear and open way. The fees charged by these mortgage brokers are often negotiable, particularly if life assurance is involved.

The right mortgage brokers have a wide range of contacts and will be able to introduce bigger investors to private banks and other specialist lenders in addition to traditional high street and clearing banks. If you decide to purchase the investment property through an offshore company for inheritance tax purposes, then it is even more important to obtain specialist mortgage advice. This is because the terms available for borrowing as an offshore company are usually considerably more expensive than buying the property and borrowing the money as an individual.

As mentioned earlier, newspapers are full of advertisements for what may seem extremely tempting mortgages for residential investment property. However, the potential investor really does need to be a specialist to understand the true costs and charges of the mortgage being advertised. As in the case of buying agents, approach two or three of the specialised brokers listed (see Useful Addresses). Their services are free of charge until you accept an offer of a mortgage arranged through them. You will quickly discover which of the mortgage brokers will provide you with the best deal and the most efficient service.

SUMMARY

◆ If you have the capital to buy one property outright, would it make sense to gear up and buy two or several properties?

◆ Decide whether to source your investment mortgage yourself or to use a specialised mortgage broker.

◆ Obtain an 'in principle' mortgage offer before making an offer on a property.

◆ Consider how long you are likely to hold the property. If you intend to add value to the property and to sell within a year or two of purchase, a variable or discounted rate will make more sense than a five- or ten-year fixed rate, which will come with a hefty penalty clause for early repayment.

CHAPTER 5

Letting and management

The most important factor when investing in residential property is deciding which property to purchase. The second most important factor is to ensure that the property lets quickly to the right tenant at full rental value and remains fully let on an annual basis while incurring the minimum amount of expenditure. Having acquired the property, the investor has three options as far as letting and management is concerned.

1. Paying a buying agent or a letting and management company to undertake all the work in connection with the letting and management of the property.
2. Employing a buying agent or a letting and management company to let the property, but then managing the property yourself.
3. Letting and managing the property yourself.

The only reason not to use the buying agent who has assisted in the purchase of the property or a separate letting and management agent is to save the cost of their fees. The cost of a full letting and management service varies across the country. It will be in the range of 10 per cent plus VAT to 17.5 per cent plus VAT of the gross rental income received each year. Taking 15 per cent as an average, 10 per cent is likely to be allocated to the letting fee and 5 per cent to the annual management fee. By saving part or all of the total average fee of 15 per cent plus VAT (ie 17.6 per cent gross) of the gross income, the actual net income received by the investor will be considerably enhanced.

Generally, both buying agents and letting and management companies operate on the same basis, as outlined below.

● They like to enter into an annual contract with the client, although they will normally accept a three-month notice clause should you decide to move the business to another agent or take it over yourself.

● They will usually collect rent on a monthly basis on the client's behalf. They should pay over to you the rent collected less deductions (see next point) within a maximum period of 21 days of having received the rent on your behalf. Most agents prefer to make rent payments by direct transfer into the client's bank account.

However, the majority of agents are also able to accommodate the individual payment preferences of the client. In the case of letting to companies rather than individuals, rent is often paid quarterly rather than monthly and therefore the net rent will be paid to the client on a quarterly basis.

● They will deduct letting and management fees plus VAT from each payment of rent to the client together with other agreed outgoings. Most agents will ask for a discretionary limit (often around £100–£150) so that they can incur some expenditure without previous written authority from the client.

● At the same time as the rent is paid into your account, the agent will send you a detailed statement of account showing precisely how the net rent has been calculated. Should there be any expenditure, then full details will also be included.

● At least once every six months in the case of properties let on a single occupancy basis, and at least once a quarter in the case of properties let on a shared basis, the agent should include with the statement of account a brief report having inspected the property on your behalf, together with any recommendations with regards to any repairs.

The Acts of Parliament that cover the laws on landlords and tenants in Scotland are different to those that apply in England and Wales. Therefore appropriate legal advice should be taken before letting and managing property in Scotland. *The Which Guide to Renting and Letting* has a useful introduction to Scottish legislation (see Further Reading).

Option 1: Using a buying agent or letting and management company throughout

If a buying agent is used to advise on the purchase of the property, the safest route is to use the same agent for the letting and management. The buying agent's reputation hinges on identifying the right property for his client and ensuring that the property is continually let to the right tenant at the maximum rental.

Some buying agents will offer guaranteed net rental returns, which can be extremely attractive to the investor. Effectively, there are three different types of so-called rental guarantee:
● a developer's rental guarantee
● a letting and management company's rental guarantee, and
● a buying agent's rental guarantee.

A developer's rental guarantee

This type of guarantee should be treated with considerable suspicion for a variety of reasons.

1. The property is often overpriced to allow for the developer's guaranteed rent.
2. The gross yields quoted in connection with such guarantees are often misleading as usually they are not calculated on the total cost of the property including acquisition fees and furnishings, and running costs such as letting and management fees are not deducted.
3. The amount of guaranteed rental may be considerably higher than the actual rental market value. This means that when the rental guarantee expires the income may drop substantially.

A letting and management company's rental guarantee

A number of letting and management companies offer rent guarantees, but their effectiveness varies. Typically, these are an insurance policy, arranged by the company, for which a premium is paid by the landlord in addition to normal management fees that covers up to three months' arrears including legal costs to recover possession.

These guarantees can give some peace of mind. However, the insurance company will insist on the most stringent vetting of the tenant before issuing the guarantee. This means that in practice the chances of arrears arising with such a tenant are slim and the cost of the guarantee simply reduces the net income received.

A buying agent's rental guarantee

Some, but by no means all, buying agents will offer investors who acquire properties through their services the choice each year of either receiving the actual net income or instead receiving a lower, but guaranteed, rental. This can be a valuable option to the investor. How it works in the case of most buying agents that offer such an arrangement is that if the anticipated net income from a property after all costs are deducted is estimated, for example, to be £10,000 each year, the buying agent will lease the property from the investor at, say, £9,000 net each year with the right to sublet. The only item that is usually excluded from such an arrangement is the cost of any repairs or alterations to the fabric of the building.

If the investor decides to take such an option from a buying agent, he should ask for a copy of the accounts of the property at the end of the first year of the guaranteed return so that he can assess how it has actually performed. He is then in a good position to decide whether to ask for a new guaranteed return at the same or higher rent the following year, or alternatively to ask for the actual net income to be paid instead of the guaranteed return.

Choosing a letting and management company

Having made the decision to use a local letting and management company, how do you choose the right one? The best way is by recommendation. If this is not an option, then study the property supplements of local newspapers and pick three letting and management companies that are offering to let similar properties to the one you have acquired for investment purposes. It is desirable, if at all possible, actually to meet the letting and management agents themselves and gauge your personal reaction to them.

There are no formal qualifications available as yet for letting and management companies, and they may or may not be controlled by a professional body. At the outset, ask to which professional body the agent belongs. The usual professional bodies are:

- Royal Institute of Chartered Surveyors (RICS)
- National Association of Estate Agents (NAEA), and
- Association of Residential Letting Agents (Arla).

All of these bodies operate a bonding scheme, which effectively means that their monies are insured and should the letting and management company, for example, go into receivership, then the owner's rental monies are protected. Unfortunately, being a member of a professional body does not necessarily mean that the agency will automatically provide a high quality service. Letting and management companies do vary enormously in their proficiency and professionalism and the only way to pick the right one is by recommendation or to interview a number of appropriate firms.

The advantages of using a buying agent or letting and management company to let and manage the property are considerable. There is a multitude of legislation and regulations to comply with when letting and managing a residential property, and it is by no means a straightforward operation. For those investors living overseas or some distance from the property they have purchased, there is really no choice – professionals should be used throughout. The alternative of using a friend or relation, unless professionally qualified, is almost always a disaster.

However, for those investors who live close to the property acquired for investment purposes and who wish to save the not inconsiderable fees involved in letting and management, then we need to look at what is involved.

Option 2: Using a buying agent or letting and management company only to let

The first point to appreciate with this option is that the saving that can be achieved by carrying out management oneself will be limited to an average of 5 per cent plus VAT (ie 5.9 per cent) of the gross rental income.

So what is involved in managing a property? The first thing is to ensure that the letting agent who has secured the tenant has drawn up the appropriate tenancy agreement, has taken a dilapidation deposit of not less than 1.25 months' rent, and has arranged for the tenants to pay the rent monthly in advance by standing order. The letting agent should also have arranged for an inventory to be prepared and to have transferred the utilities and Council Tax to the tenant's name. Avoid the temptation to cut costs by preparing your own inventory. Invariably it will be inferior to the inventory prepared by a professional agent and could be later seen as being biased in the event of any legal dispute. As you are managing the property, you will need to ensure that the letting agent hands over the dilapidation deposit to you together with the signed tenancy agreement and the completed inventory.

To put it in its simplest terms, management of the property then involves the following.

1. Ensuring that the rent is paid in full by the tenant on the due date.
2. Ensuring that the property is kept in a good state of repair. If any repair is required due to the tenant's misuse, then the obligation to organise and pay for the repair falls to the tenant.
3. Ensuring that outgoings are paid by the landlord or tenant, as appropriate.
4. Ensuring that the garden is maintained by either the landlord or the tenant as specifically agreed at the commencement of the tenancy.
5. Knowing what to do at the end of the tenancy.

Ensuring payment of the rent
In order to ensure that the rent is paid in full by the tenant and on the due date, it is of considerable benefit to get to know the tenant on a personal level and to form a good relationship from the outset. In the event of the rent not being paid within seven days of the date it was due, the best way forward is to telephone the tenant and ask what the problem is. Arrears only become a problem if they are allowed to build up. If the reason for non-payment is a genuine mistake, for example if a tenant's bank has inadvertently cancelled the standing order, then the tenant will swiftly remedy the situation. If the rent has been withheld because the tenant is unhappy that a requested repair has not be attended to, then the matter can be resolved at an early stage. If the tenant has not paid the rent because of some personal problem such as losing his job, then you should discuss the situation openly with the tenant.

Do remember that for the first month of the arrears there is the protection of the 1.25 months' dilapidation deposit, whereas after the end of that 1.25 months there is no guarantee that the rent arrears will be recovered. The best way to resolve these situations is always by negotiation with the tenant; only if all else fails should a solicitor be consulted. An eviction will automatically be granted by the court if there are two months' arrears at the time the order is sought. If this is necessary, legal advice should be sought immediately. It should be remembered that harassment and/or unlawful eviction are criminal offences and the tenant may also have access to civil remedies. Details of what constitutes harassment or unlawful eviction are incorporated in the Protection from Eviction Act of 1977 and in the Criminal Law Act of 1977.

Keeping the property in a good state of repair

Managing the property also involves ensuring that it is well maintained. If a drain becomes blocked or the roof starts to leak, the tenant will contact you and ask you to remedy the fault. If you do not do so promptly, then the tenant is likely to withhold rent. We have already looked in detail at the importance of only buying a property for investment purposes which has been comprehensively refurbished, is refurbished immediately after purchase, or is brand new or modern. Even so, maintenance problems do arise.

Who is responsible if the roof starts leaking or if the central heating develops a fault? It is important that the landlord and tenant have a comprehensive tenancy agreement drawn up by the buying agent or the letting and management company. However, various Acts of Parliament can overrule the terms of any specific tenancy agreements. Basically, under the Landlord and Tenant Act of 1985, the landlord's obligations are:

● to keep in repair the structure and exterior of the property including drains, gutters and external pipes

● to keep in repair and in proper working order the installations in the property of the supply of water, electricity, gas and sanitation including all basins, sinks, baths and sanitary conveniences, and

● to keep in repair and in proper working order the installations in the property for room and water heating.

For those who have chosen to manage the property themselves, *The Which Guide to Renting and Letting* (see Further Reading) provides a useful and detailed guide to the considerable amount of legislation and common law relating to both landlords' and tenants' obligations in respect of repairs to the property.

It is important that the landlord physically inspects the property about once every quarter. When making the quarterly inspection, the property should be physically checked both inside and out. This inspection should include in particular a check as to whether any of the gutters are blocked and whether there are any obvious signs of leaks either through the roof or from shower trays, etc. It is equally important that the investor arranges to meet the tenants to check that they are happy. Happy tenants mean a trouble-free property investment. Unhappy tenants mean problems.

In addition to the investor's obligation to maintain a property in good repair, there are now stringent regulations concerning furnishings (see Chapter 6), gas, electrical equipment, and fire and safety that apply to all properties that are let for investment purposes.

Gas installation and appliance safety

This is regulated by the Gas Safety (Installation and Use) Regulations of 1994 and the Gas Safety (Installation and Use) (Amendment) Regulations of 1996. These regulations operate under the jurisdiction of the Health and Safety at Work Act of 1974. One section in particular covers the responsibilities of landlords and specifies the following.

- A safety check must be made at least once a year by a gas installer registered with the Council of Registered Gas Installers (Corgi) and approved by the Health and Safety Executive (HSE) for this purpose. (The cost of servicing and certification usually depends on the amount of work and travel involved, but is usually between £40 and £100.)
- Certificates of inspection must be obtained and copies given to each tenant whether they ask for them or not. Records must be kept for at least two years.
- The certificate must show that all gas appliances including boilers, hobs, tumble dryers, cookers, and all installation pipework together with flues have been checked and there has been an examination of: a) the effectiveness of any flue; b) the supply of combustion air; c) operating pressure and heat output; and d) operation to ensure safe functioning.

Carbon monoxide is a highly poisonous gas and has no colour, no smell and no taste, so it is difficult to recognise. Tell-tale signs that an appliance is not working properly are staining, sooting or discoloration on or around the appliance, a yellow or orange flame instead of the normal blue, or a pilot light that keeps going out.

Between 40 and 50 people die each year from carbon monoxide poisoning caused by poorly installed or faulty gas appliances. Apart from the fact that the landlord would be open to criminal prosecution and civil proceedings, no one would like to feel in any way responsible for the loss of a person's life through negligence.

In December 1997, a landlord and a workman were imprisoned after admitting responsibility for the death of a student tenant who was killed by poisonous fumes from a faulty gas boiler – the first custodial sentences for a case of this sort. The landlord was jailed for two years, while the workman received an 18-month sentence for what the judge described as gross negligence.

Electrical installation and appliance safety

The Electrical Equipment (Safety) Regulations of 1994 impose an obligation on the landlord to ensure that all electrical installations and appliances are safe, will not cause danger and will satisfy safety requirements. In addition, appropriate instructions must be supplied to the users of the equipment.

To comply with the obligations and to protect the landlord, an annual check of all electrical installations and appliances by a competent electrician is recommended. Records of such inspections should be kept. There is no statutory guidance for safety testing, but visual inspection by a competent person can detect the vast majority of electrical problems. The electrician should check that:

● live parts are not accessible
● leads are not worn or frayed and are complete, with no joints
● correct plugs to BS 1363 standard are fitted and correctly fused (for 220–240 volt equipment, typical fuse ratings are: up to 750 watts – 3 amp; up to 1,250 watts – 5 amp; above 1,250 watts – 13 amp); fuses to BS 13652 standard should be used throughout
● any moving parts should be guarded
● electric blankets should be serviced according to manufacturers' instructions
● microwave doors should be clean, free from erosion and effective
● washing machines, cookers etc, should be serviced and in good working order
● electric heaters and central heating appliances should be serviced annually, and
● electrical garden equipment should be used with a residual current device to BS 7071 standard.

Smoke alarms

The Building Regulations of 1991 state that all properties built since June 1992 must be fitted with mains-powered, inter-linked smoke detectors/alarms. It is recommended that at least battery-operated smoke alarms are fitted in all investment properties, whenever built, as the chances of surviving a house fire are two to three times greater with an alarm. A property investor could be civilly liable in the event of injury or death by fire if smoke detectors are not fitted in a property, whenever it was built. So, it is important to ensure that:

● the smoke detectors fitted are to the BS 6446 standard, which will ensure the alarm's sensitivity to smoke
● if any of the alarms are in a position that is difficult to reach, a smoke detector with a 'torch test' feature is fitted
● if there are likely to be false alarms (for example, in the kitchen), an alarm is fitted with a mute button that desensitises the alarm temporarily, and
● if you can afford it, an interlinked mains alarm rather than battery-powered alarms is choosen as they all sound if just one of them senses smoke and therefore give the best protection.

The exact siting of smoke detectors depends on the following points.

- Have at least one on every floor and extra alarms in rooms where fires are likely to start (for example, the kitchen).
- Position carefully according to the instructions and in an area of maximum air circulation to give the earliest possible warning.
- Take account of the audibility of the alarms, particularly from within the bedrooms.

Failure to comply with safety legislation is a criminal offence. An offence carries a punishment of imprisonment or a Level 5 fine, which is currently £5,000, or both. These penalties are only for non-compliance. In addition, a landlord could be held liable and subject to much greater penalties should an injury or death occur. These rules and regulations are, quite rightly, comprehensive and it is essential that they are complied with.

Ensuring that all outgoings are paid

If a buying agent or a letting and management company is not used to manage the property, it will be the owner's responsibility to ensure that all bills are paid. The letting agent should have arranged for gas and electricity meters to be read at the commencement of the tenancy and the relevant service provider notified of the change of occupier. It is essential that accounts are put in the name of the tenants from the commencement of the tenancy. Water rates are paid by the tenant if the supply is metered. Telephone, including reconnection charges, are entirely the tenant's responsibility and the account should be in the tenant's name. At the end of the tenancy it is important that the tenant has notified the telephone company in advance of the date when the telephone should be disconnected and that the tenant's account is settled and closed.

As regards the Council Tax, the tenant, under the Local Government Finance Act of 1992, is obliged to pay this (the exception is a house wholly occupied by students, which is not subject to Council Tax) and indemnify the landlord against any liability for this charge. It is the landlord's responsibility to insure the building and the contents that he has provided and to comply with the insurance company's security requirements. However, it is up to the tenant to take out his own insurance to cover personal possessions. The landlord should provide a set of keys to the property for each occupant and these must be returned by the tenants at the end of the tenancy.

Garden maintenance

If the property has a garden, it should be tidy and have a mown lawn at the start of the tenancy. The garden should be designed in such a way to ensure that maintenance will be as low as possible. The landlord should provide basic garden tools including a mower in good working order so that the tenant is encouraged to look after the garden during the tenancy. If the house is let to students or professionals as a shared house, the ideal arrangement is to have a small paved garden with no grass. Precise obligations for maintaining the garden and supplied equipment must be ascertained at the outset and an appropriate clause written into the tenancy agreement.

At the end of a tenancy

It is important that the tenant agrees to provide the landlord with access to the property by arrangement for at least the last six weeks of the tenancy in order that prospective new tenants can be shown round. Otherwise, unless it is a genuine emergency, the landlord must not enter the property without first informing the tenant by reasonable prior notice.

It is very important that the landlord obtains a forwarding address for outgoing tenants, especially if part of the deposit has been retained against expenditure/outstanding bills. The point of this dilapidation deposit is so that the landlord can retain part of it to cover any outstanding bills, and also to rectify any damage and pay for any breakages.

It must be remembered, however, that legally bills remain the responsibility of the tenant, not the landlord. The cleaning of carpets, curtains, blankets etc, may be charged to the tenant if the inventory clerk considers that they have not been professionally cleaned in accordance with the tenancy agreement.

Option 3: Letting and managing the property yourself

To carry out personally both letting and management will save the investor an average of 15 per cent plus VAT (ie 17.6 per cent) of the gross rental income received.

So, having described what is involved in managing the property yourself, we now need to look at what is involved in letting the property as well.

The following matters need to be attended to when letting the property.

1. Preparation of the property.
2. Selecting the type of tenant: single occupancy or as a shared property; professionals or students.
3. Rent assessment committees.
4. Marketing.
5. Tenant selection.
6. Tenancy agreements.
7. Inventory and Schedule of Condition.

Preparation of the property

A decision has to be made as to which equipment works satisfactorily, whether more appliances are needed, what decoration needs to be carried out and what furnishings need replacing to ensure the maximum rental return. To answer these questions a decision has to be made at the outset as to what type of tenant is going to be targeted to rent the property. Clearly a property needs to be decorated and furnished to an entirely different standard if it is to be let to students than if it is to be let to a high income professional family.

Market research needs to be carried out at the outset to ascertain the most suitable type of tenant for the property in order to provide the highest return. The biggest decision to make is whether to let the property as a single occupancy to, for example, a professional couple or a family, or to let the property as a shared house.

Single occupancy

A single occupancy tenancy is usually the most trouble-free and incurs the minimum amount of wear, tear and maintenance. The type of tenant will obviously depend on whether the property is, say, a small one-bedroom flat or a large detached house with five bedrooms and two bathrooms, but the principles are the same.

In many towns and cities there is excellent demand from single occupancy tenants for well located and well presented accommodation and the average tenancy period is usually nine to twelve months. Obviously, if a tenant can be found who wishes, in principle, to stay for two to three years then that is excellent, but in this situation provision should be built into the tenancy agreement to review the rent upwards at the end of each year. As is covered in Chapter 6, single occupancy tenants increasingly require property to be part-furnished only, which once again is to the advantage of the landlord.

Letting as a shared house

What does letting as a shared house actually mean? It means letting to a number of individuals, usually between three and six people, who are not a family but who occupy the property in the same way as a family sharing the kitchen, bathroom and sitting-room facilities. Letting properties as individual bedsits is quite different as this means that each room let has its own kitchen and although bathrooms may be shared, there is usually no communal sitting-room. Letting a property as bedsits is fraught with difficulties and is not recommended to investors in residential property.

There are two choices when making a property available to let as a shared house: either let to young professionals or let to students. The first golden rule is that students and young professionals should not be mixed. Generally such groups fail to get on well. In addition, complications will arise in respect of Council Tax. A property let as a shared house entirely to students is exempt from Council Tax, whereas a house let to professionals sharing is liable to the tax. If there are one or more students sharing a house with professionals, they will become liable for Council Tax which, understandably, they will not wish to pay. Given that the students will expect to be exempt, the obligation will inevitably fall on the landlord.

The reason why so many people let properties on a shared basis is quite simply that the total rental received can be up to 30 per cent to 40 per cent higher than if the property is let on a single occupancy basis. Tenant selection and management becomes even more vital when letting a house on a shared basis, but if done correctly it works extremely well.

Letting a shared house to professionals

This works well in many towns and cities across the country. If you take as an example a three-bedroom town house, then such a property might let for approximately £800 per month on a single occupancy basis. However, by using the front reception room (it is essential, of course, whether the house is old or new, that there is a separate entrance hallway) as a fourth bedroom, the property should work well if let to four professional sharers. If the four professionals are each paying around £260 per month exclusive of bills, then the gross rental received by the landlord will be £1,040 per calendar month as opposed to £800.

There are additional rules and regulations relating to the letting of shared houses. However, in most cases, these are relatively easy to comply with. One of the most important regulations is that no bedroom should be less than approximately 6.5 square metres, which rules out some houses where the third bedroom is too small.

The property should be advertised as being suitable for sharers and ideally they should make up their own group. If the house has four bedrooms and a group of three individuals say they are interested in the property, then it is best to ask them to find a fourth person to share so that they are confident they will get on with each other. Professionals sharing together is becoming increasingly popular and it is surprising how few problems there are with groups not getting on together – tolerance between young people is surprisingly high.

References should be taken out on each tenant in the usual way (see page 129) and it is customary to have a separate lease for each professional. An important point is that all four tenancies should start on the same date and ideally end on the same date.

Alternatively, a single lease should be entered into, preferably on a joint and several basis. Lets to professional sharers are usually for a 12-month period.

In London, in particular, there is a big market for letting two-bedroom flats to sharers where a third person has a bed in the sitting-room. Once again, this can work well from both the landlord's and tenant's points of views. If each tenant pays, for example, £350 per month, this is still likely to be well below the cost of renting a studio flat for single occupation or paying for bed and breakfast accommodation. Also, to many young professionals it is much more appealing to live with two or three like-minded individuals than to live alone.

Letting a shared house to students

Letting to students sounds a dangerous idea to some first-time investors in residential property, but as long as certain rules are strictly adhered to it works extremely well. As in the case of letting to young professionals, a shared house needs to be fully furnished and equipped, the house should be clean, tidy and well presented, but the quality of the furnishings need be no higher than average.

The first point to consider when letting to students is the importance of the academic year. There is a market for professionals to share at any time of year, while for obvious reasons the peak time to let to students is at the commencement of the academic year in September/October. There is a market from students throughout the rest of the year, but it is much weaker. Therefore, if market research shows that the demand for a particular house is going to be from students and the property is bought in January, the best plan is to let the property on a short-term lease up to the end of August/September to any tenant available who is acceptable from a reference point of view.

Although common practice varies from university city to university city, the most common arrangement is that students take a property for a full 12-month period but will only pay half-rent during August and September. This means that the property is let throughout the year, although the students will not normally physically be in occupation for two months over the summer. This gives the landlord time to carry out any maintenance works required. Alternatively, particularly in cities such as Edinburgh, maximum returns can be made from letting for a 10-month period and then to let the property as short-term holiday accommodation (for example, for the Edinburgh festival during the months of July and August when substantial rents can be generated). Letting a property as short-term holiday accommodation is a specialised business and UNiSkiLL Ltd provides a comprehensive book on the subject (see Further Reading).

In most of the large university cities there is huge demand from students for suitable accommodation from the start of the academic year. The key to success when it comes to letting to students is to choose the right ones. What this means is that, ideally:

- they should be postgraduates and not undergraduates, and
- their parents should agree to pay the rent by standing order.

On the first point, undergraduates can make good tenants, but should be carefully vetted by interview. On the second point, if the students themselves agree to pay the rent by standing order and their rent is guaranteed in writing by their parents, then this is also acceptable. In this case it is essential that the parents are resident in the United Kingdom, as guarantees from parents who are resident overseas are usually worthless.

In addition, as a 'belt and braces' situation, it is worth considering making the tenancies joint and several. In other words, if the property is let to four students, then one lease should be drawn up making each of the four students responsible for the whole rent. In this case, if one student defaults the remaining three are responsible for the defaulter's rent. However, in the situation where parents are paying the rent direct, this is unnecessary and inappropriate.

If letting to students is only carried out as advised above, then problems will be relatively few and far between. The property should be inspected at least once a quarter to ensure that it is being properly maintained. As usual, a full dilapidation deposit, ideally 1.5 months' rent, will be taken to protect against undue wear and tear or damage. In practice most students, while extremely untidy, will look after properties fairly well, particularly if those properties are well presented in the first instance.

Rules and regulations relating specifically to shared houses

There is considerable legislation and a multitude of rules and regulations that attempt to define whether or not a house is let as a shared house (ie a house in multiple occupation – an HMO). If there is any doubt, then advice should be sought from the Environmental Health Officer and from the Housing Officer of the appropriate city council. Generally, it is safe to assume that if a house is let to three or more people who are not from the same family, then the house is an HMO. The following are purely some guidelines as to the rules and regulations pertaining to shared houses. However, as requirements do vary from city to city, it is important to check with the local council.

1. It is normally necessary to register the property as an HMO with the city council for which a small one-off fee is usually charged.
2. If letting to four sharers, then one bathroom or shower room is sufficient.
3. If letting to five sharers, then there should be a separate WC in addition to the bathroom or shower room.
4. If letting to six sharers, then there must be two bathrooms or shower rooms including two separate WCs. There must also be two cookers and two fridges.

5. No planning permission is required to let a property out as a shared house provided the house is occupied by a maximum of six people.

6. If the property is to be let to more than six persons, then planning permission is required. In most towns and cities the granting of such planning permission is strongly resisted by the planning department.

7. If the property is just on two floors, then it is subject to the same fire and safety rules and regulations as a house under ordinary occupation.

8. If the house is arranged on three floors (for example, because the roof space has been converted into a fourth bedroom), then additional fire and safety regulations need to be complied with. Details of these will be supplied by the local council, but in almost all cases they will involve the provision of emergency lighting, and a mains-powered smoke and fire detection system. They will also involve a protected staircase, either by enclosing the staircase with a lobby or by ensuring that relevant doors have appropriate fire resistance. Investors should be aware that the cost of complying with additional fire and safety regulations on a house designed on three floors and let as an HMO can amount to several thousand pounds. At the time of publication of this book, grants are still available to assist with the works required in this regard, but it is thought that such grants may well be phased out over the next year or two. Details of grants are available from the Housing Officer of the local council.

Rent assessment committees

Since the Housing Act of 1996, it is no longer necessary for an assured shorthold tenancy to be for a fixed term. However, when a tenancy is granted for a fixed term the tenant can, during the first six months of that term, apply to the local rent assessment committee for a determination of the rent which, in the committee's opinion, the landlord might reasonably be expected to obtain under the shorthold tenancy. There is no question that the rent could be assessed at a level lower than the market rent for the premises – this is not a return to the 'fair rent' system used under the Rent Act of 1977. Instead, the purpose of this legislation is to stop landlords charging unwitting tenants more than the open market value rent.

In practice, not many people apply to rent assessment committees to have their rent reviewed because:

● most tenants have an idea of open market rent and will not pay more, and

● the right to have rent reduced by the rent assessment committee must, by law, be referred to in the assured shorthold tenancy, but most tenants are, one suspects, unaware of their rights in this respect.

It is worth remembering that the rent assessment committee cannot make such a determination unless there is a sufficient number of similar houses in the locality let on assured tenancies to suggest a normal open market rent and unless the rent payable under the shorthold tenancy is in fact significantly higher than the open market rent.

Bearing this in mind, the investor, whether letting on a single occupancy or a shared house basis, should resist any temptation to charge more than the open market rent. Usually, tenants will eventually discover that they are paying over the odds. This will make them disgruntled and hence less obliging as tenants. There is also the risk that they will appeal to a rent assessment committee and that the rent will be reduced.

When a property is let as a shared house, a specific point needs to be made with regard to a joint and several tenancy. In a recent case in Cambridge, the local rent assessment committee decided that a property let to five students at £1,000 per month on a joint and several tenancy lease should have the rent reduced to £800 – the average open market rent if the property was let as a single occupancy tenancy. The rent assessment committee did not disagree with the fact that the rents charged per room were the market norm, but because there was only one lease they held that the open market rent should be judged as what the house would fetch if let on a single occupancy tenancy. Other rent assessment committees may not hold the same view, but investors should weigh up the advantages of the security of a joint and secured lease against the risk of the rent being reduced by a rent assessment committee.

Marketing the property

Having decided on the type of tenant required, there are four ways to advertise the availability of the property.

1. Erect a board outside the property advertising that the property is to let. There is no reason why a private individual cannot erect a 'to let' board with a telephone number on it, and not only is it a cheap way of advertising but also it is one of the most effective ways of advertising a property to let. However, in many cities and towns there are specific regulations about the erection of 'to let' boards and this needs to be checked with the local council beforehand as there are usually restrictions on the size and number of boards permitted.

2. Place an advertisement in the local newspaper. You will soon see that most local newspapers have a wide variety of properties to let at any one time. A low-cost lineage advertisement is usually sufficient, but for properties with a rental value of over £1,000 a month a display advertisement with a photograph will usually produce good results.

3. Mailshot universities, colleges, hospitals and other major local employers. All of these institutions will have accommodation officers and this route is often successful.
4. Mailshot relocation agents. Increasingly, relocation agents are being employed by larger companies to seek rented accommodation, especially at the higher end of the market, for their employees and so are often an excellent source of high quality tenants. The difficulty is that relocation agents are unlikely to be based locally and therefore you will need to approach all the main relocation agents. (For further details, see Useful Addresses.)

At least two months before the end of the tenancy, approach the tenant in writing or by telephone to ascertain whether he wishes to renew the tenancy. If he does, this is the time to negotiate an increase in the rental if market conditions allow. If the tenant does not wish to renew the tenancy then it is essential that the marketing of the property starts at least six weeks before the end of the tenancy period. The aim must always be to obtain 100 per cent occupancy and this is certainly feasible two years out of every three. In the third year it is usually necessary to have possession of the property for at least one week for thorough cleaning, internal redecorating and any repairs. All the examples in this book provide for a void period of one month every year. While it is sensible to allow for this when calculating your anticipated net return from an investment property, in practice you should usually be able to do a lot better.

Tenant selection
Once a tenant is found, a character reference, a previous landlord reference and a reference from a bank or employer should be obtained as evidence that the tenant is able to afford the rent. Even better is a reference from a credit referencing company (see Useful Addresses). Although they make a small charge for this, it does mean that the reference can be relied on more. In the case of a company let, a general enquiry as to the status of the company should be adequate, although remember that companies can, and do, go bust.

Drawing up a tenancy agreement
The next step is to draw up an appropriate tenancy agreement. In most circumstances this will be an Assured Shorthold Tenancy. The tenancy agreement is drawn up to cover present day legislation to protect the investor's interest and to give the tenant clear instructions as to his duties and responsibilities.

Basic tenancy agreements can be bought from a law stationers but, unless the investor has real knowledge of the subject, it is advisable to have it prepared by someone who has knowledge of the landlord and tenant laws. Although solicitors seem an obvious choice for this, they are expensive. A quicker and cheaper route is to approach a local letting and management agent and ask them if they would advise on the terms of the lease for a small one-off fee.

Inventories and Schedules of Condition

A detailed inventory (ie a list of all items of furniture, fixtures and fittings, and equipment supplied by the landlord) should be prepared and signed by both the tenant and the landlord prior to the commencement of the tenancy. A Schedule of Condition should also be prepared so there is no argument with the tenant as to the current state of decoration. Ideally the tenant should agree to give up the property at the end of the tenancy, allowing for fair wear and tear, in no worse a condition than at the commencement of the tenancy. Any remedial work required to bring it back up to that condition should be carried out at the expense of the tenant.

It is important that a dilapidation deposit of more than one month is agreed on. The problem with asking for only one month's deposit is that an unscrupulous tenant will fail to pay the last month's rent and will then disappear at the end of the tenancy. If there are items that need to be deducted from the deposit, either in respect of repairs or outstanding bills, then there will be no deposit left from which to deduct these amounts. Ideally a deposit of 1.5 months should be insisted upon, although 1.25 months is usually adequate. Tenants should be asked to pay rent in advance by standing order on the first day of each month. This allows the landlord to check quickly and easily if the rent has been received by his bank.

Support and advice

For those investors who do decide to let and manage their properties themselves, it may be worth joining the Small Landlords Association (see Useful Addresses).

It is also useful to know that private landlords can now use the services of an independent Housing Ombudsman in the case of disputes with tenants instead of going to law. In early 1998, the Housing Ombudsman is Roger Jeffries (see Useful Addresses) and he will arbitrate on disputes between landlords and tenants. This is often far more effective and far cheaper than going through the courts.

SUMMARY

◆ After due consideration, make a clear decision as to whether you are going to use professionals to let and manage the property, whether you will use them to let the property only and then manage it yourself, or whether you will both let and manage the property yourself.

◆ If you decide to use professional help and you have used a buying agent to advise on the purchase of the property, they are likely to provide the best service for letting and managing the property. If the buying agent is not to be used, then interview a minimum of three local letting and management companies that specialise in letting and managing properties similar to the one you have acquired for investment.

◆ If you decide to undertake all or part of the letting and management process yourself, be prepared to spend time familiarising yourself with the basic landlord and tenant rules and regulations, on market research and on the actual letting and management process.

◆ Do not ask a friend or relative to look after the management or letting. It is not only unfair to the friend or relative, but usually produces highly unsatisfactory results.

◆ Managing property is largely about managing people. Unhappy tenants will immediately create problems.

◆ If you decide to let the property yourself, aim to achieve 100 per cent occupancy for two years out of every three-year cycle and 95 per cent occupancy in the third year. If you are employing a professional letting agent, consider offering him an annual bonus for achieving these occupancy rates when negotiating his fee.

CHAPTER 6

Furnishing

When it comes to furnishing your investment property, there are three choices: not to furnish at all, to part furnish, or to fully furnish. Once this decision is made and the answer is to part furnish or fully furnish the property, the next question is to what standard it should be furnished.

If buying agents are used, then they will advise on all these matters but will charge for the advice and for arranging the furnishing of the property. Charges levied by buying agents vary but typically average around 12.5 per cent of the cost of furnishing. This may will be charged either as an additional project management fee plus VAT, or it will be incorporated into the cost of the furnishing package.

All competent letting and management companies will advise on the furnishings required to maximise rental. However, relatively few will actually organise the purchase and installation of the furnishings.

If you decide to do without professional help, then the decision as to what degree of furnishing is required needs to be made early on. One first point to grasp is that, rather confusingly, a part furnished property is often referred to as unfurnished property by letting and management companies. The market for a literally unfurnished property (ie no carpets, no curtains and no appliances) is virtually non-existent and so this option should be discounted from the outset.

When agents refer to unfurnished properties, they invariably mean part furnished to include fitted carpets, curtains and all or some white goods (ie cooker, fridge, washing machine and sometimes dishwasher). Fully furnished means just that – the property is completely furnished and ready to move into as it includes all necessary furniture, appliances (but not usually television and stereo), kitchen equipment and bedding (ie blankets, duvets and pillows, but usually not linen).

Part furnishing a property

Particularly in the last year or two there has been a considerable increase in the demand for part furnished properties as opposed to fully furnished properties and, with the exception of properties let as shared houses or flats, this is becoming the norm. There used to be a rental differential of between 10 per cent and 20 per cent between part and fully furnished properties, but this has now disappeared in most cities and towns. In fact, there is evidence in some cities, particularly London, that there is greater demand for part furnished properties as opposed to those that are fully furnished.

This is a considerable advantage to the investor as the cost of part furnishing is generally around 50 per cent of the cost of fully furnishing and obviously there is then 50 per cent less depreciation. However, in making the decision whether to part furnish or fully furnish, one should also bear in mind the loss of tax privileges that are attached to letting fully furnished (see Chapter 7).

The best way to get a feel for how to present a part furnished property to the maximum advantage is to look at several properties currently on the local rental market. Ask the letting agents for those properties about the ideal standard of equipment to be provided for that particular location.

Fixtures and fittings

In part furnished properties, although tenants will provide their own furniture, it is still advisable to provide fixtures such as towel rails, coat rails and picture hooks. The alternative – that tenants provide their own but then remove them at the end of the tenancy – results in holes throughout the house, which then create extra work because they have to be filled and redecorated.

The quality of the curtains and carpets will of course depend on the quality of the property, but the golden rule is that the better a property is presented at the commencement of the tenancy, the more likely the tenants will treat the property in a careful and considerate way.

How to decorate

It is advisable to paint rather than wallpaper the walls unless the property is of particularly high value (ie a rental value of over £650 per week in London and over £400 per week elsewhere). For most levels of rent, the walls should be painted throughout in a neutral colour to complement the colour of the carpets.

The most standard colour scheme used is magnolia walls and white ceilings which, while not inspiring, is inoffensive and has the advantage that it will go with the majority of furnishings and also with varnished wooden floors, which have now become so popular with tenants, particularly in London.

Carpets and curtains

Carpets should always be plain and not patterned, and of reasonable quality. Even low priced carpets must have proper underlay, as foam backed carpets cannot be steam-cleaned and always have a short life span. Carpets should not be put in bathrooms. It is far better to have tiles or linoleum in bathrooms as well as in kitchens.

Hand-made curtains are expensive and it is far better to buy something that is ready-made other than for the most expensive properties. Curtains should be chosen to enhance the general colour scheme, but should be plain rather than over-adventurous.

White goods

Do not be tempted to buy second-hand, so-called 'guaranteed' fridges, cookers or washing machines when letting for the first time. These invariably give trouble and in the long term frequently cost far more both in terms of money and time expended than providing reasonable quality new white goods.

Offering both part and fully furnished options

Initially, only furnish the property to a part furnished standard (unless letting as a shared house) as you always have the option of providing all furnishings if that is what a particularly good tenant requires. It is sensible, therefore, when advertising the property to describe it as being part or fully furnished at the option of the tenant. If you decide to fully furnish and then discover that the best tenant only requires the property to be part furnished, you have wasted what could amount to several thousand pounds of capital expenditure.

Fully furnishing a property

There are a number of specialist companies that provide a full- or part-furnishing package for people buying properties for investment purposes. Details of some of these companies will be found in Useful Addresses. It is worth obtaining a quotation from one or more of these companies as, even if they are not used, their schedules can provide a useful checklist to ensure that no items are overlooked, and the quotations are also useful for comparing costs.

When letting properties on a shared basis, either to professionals or to students, they will need to be fully furnished and equipped. A guide figure to fully furnish and equip a fairly small three-bedroom house let on a shared basis is around £8,600. Expect to be charged around £10,000 if using a buying agent or a letting and management company to do all the work.

All furniture should be solid and well made, but functional rather than decorative. Avoid shower curtains as these become stained and unsightly rather quickly. Instead fit shower screens whenever possible. Bathrooms in shared houses get a lot of use, and condensation is often a major problem. It is therefore essential to provide an extractor fan, even when the bathroom has a window.

A fully furnished property let to students or professionals does not need pictures on the walls, and tenants of most properties usually prefer to buy their own coffee tables and other items which will give a more homely feel to the property. However, when fully furnishing a high value property for single occupancy it is important to provide all such items, including pictures, and to do everything possible to give the property a homely and welcoming feel. Although you will have researched carefully and acquired a property in a location where the letting market is strong, at the same time you must always remember that there is usually considerable competition. So, when letting on a single occupancy basis, small finishing touches (including providing one or two potted plants and making sure that the property is spotlessly clean right down to the windows), can make all the difference between getting an early let at maximum rent and having to show a property many times over before securing a satisfactory let at only an average rental. As the rental market grows tenants are becoming more discerning and this is particularly true of high rental properties (ie over £2,000 per month in London, and over £1,000 per month elsewhere).

Furniture and furnishings safety

The Furniture and Furnishings (Fire) (Safety) Regulations introduced in 1988 made it an offence to supply in the course of business any furniture that does not pass the 'cigarette test'. To pass this test, furniture should not catch fire if a burning cigarette is left lying on the fabric. In 1993, amended regulations set new levels of fire resistance for upholstered furniture and furnishings.

Furniture purchased since March 1990 is likely to comply and should have an appropriate label attached. It is vital that all furniture is checked for these labels. Furniture manufactured before 1 January 1950 does not need to comply as defective materials were not used prior to this date. These regulations apply to items such as beds, mattresses, headboards, pillows, scatter cushions, bean bags, prams, nursery furniture, outdoor furniture, loose covers, suites, upholstered furniture and other similar items. It does not apply to carpets and curtains, bedclothes (including duvets) and sleeping bags.

A guide to the Furnishings and Furnishings (Fire) (Safety) Regulations is produced by the Department of Trade and Industry and is obtainable from the Consumer Safety Unit (see Further Reading).

SUMMARY

◆ Whether you decide to part furnish or fully furnish, it is essential to comply with current regulations.

◆ Fully furnishing attracts valuable tax benefits which are not available when only part furnishing (for details, see Chapter 7).

◆ Do not be tempted to use second-hand appliances and equipment. Start with new equipment throughout.

◆ If in any doubt as to whether to part or fully furnish, then only part furnish and advertise the property as being available on either a part or fully furnished basis at the option of the tenant.

◆ When letting properties on a shared basis, properties must be fully furnished to a good average standard.

◆ When letting on a single occupancy basis, greater care must be taken to make the property as welcoming and attractive as possible. This often involves thought and time rather than a material amount of additional expenditure. Remember, to you the property is an investment, but to the tenant it's home!

CHAPTER 7

Taxation

Although often the last consideration for many people, the tax implications of buying a property to let should not be overlooked. Many accountants are not familiar with the ways of minimising tax in respect of the income and capital gains that accrue from an investment in residential property. It is therefore sensible to seek advice from a specialist firm (see Useful Addresses), with this being particularly relevant if you are a non-resident of the United Kingdom, or perhaps a non-domiciliary.

Landlords resident in the UK

Under current legislation, most rental income, regardless of the type of lease, is pooled together. Therefore, a loss on a furnished property may be offset against profits on an unfurnished property, and vice versa. However, this excludes holiday lettings which are covered later in this chapter.

Income tax

In preparation for self-assessment, the taxation rules for rental income were changed in April 1995 with the intention of simplifying the basis of assessment and bringing furnished and unfurnished lettings together under the single heading of the 'business of letting' (Schedule A). Previously unfurnished letting was assessed under Schedule A, while furnished letting was dealt with under Schedule D. Unfurnished letting income was taxed on a 'preceding years' basis, while furnished letting was assessed on a 'current year' basis. The new rules now mean that after a transitional period, all such income can be declared and taxed on the more comprehensive current year basis.

What this all means is that ownership of investment property, even if it is just one property, is now treated as a business by the Inland Revenue. As a result, this creates significant tax advantages. In particular, the following are now deductible from the taxable profit:

- all interest payments on a loan taken out to purchase or improve the property
- travel and other ancillary expenses wholly and exclusively incurred for the purpose of the business
- the fees of a buying agent or letting and management company

- the accountancy costs incurred in connection with the preparation of annual accounts
- expenses in respect to water rates, repairs, maintenance, insurance etc, and
- certain expenses incurred prior to letting the property.

In addition, for a property that is fully furnished, the investor can claim an allowance for wear and tear on furnishings. This is calculated on the basis of 10 per cent of the annual rental income less water rates and Council Tax (if paid by the investor). Alternatively, the investor can claim for the replacement cost, but in most cases the 10 per cent allowance is both more beneficial and straightforward. Unfortunately, properties that are part furnished or fully unfurnished do not obtain this tax relief.

The earnings basis

It should be remembered that, as a business, the Inland Revenue will expect the 'earnings basis' to be applied. In other words, it is necessary to ignore income that is due outside the tax year and include all income that actually has been paid. Similarly, expenses are deductible in the period for which they were incurred and not when the invoice was issued or paid.

For example, if a landlord rents out his property for £1,250 per calendar month during 1998, payable on the first of each month, the total annual rent for 1998 is £15,000. Then if, in 1999, he rents out the same property for an increased rent of £1,500 per calendar month, the total annual rent will be £18,000.

However for the purposes of the Inland Revenue, his income for the 1998/99 tax year (beginning of April to end of March) will be nine months at £1,250 plus three months at £1,500. Therefore the total taxable income for the 1998/99 tax year will be £15,750.

Equally, only expenses for the 1998/99 tax year are deductible. So, using the same example, an item such as insurance, which is paid annually on 1 January, has to be claimed proportionally. If the insurance payment made on 1 January 1998 is £500 and the subsequent payment made on 1 January 1999 is £600, the amount that is allowable for the 1998/99 tax year will be three-quarters of the £500 payment (April through to December) plus one-quarter of the £600 payment (January through to March). The total insurance expense would therefore be £525.

As is illustrated, some knowledge of accountancy principles are required to determine accurately income and outgoings. In addition, with the introduction of self-assessment in April 1996, the onus to reach the right conclusion has been pushed even further in the direction of the taxpayer. Some relief is provided in that when gross receipts from the rental business do not exceed £15,000, the investor is permitted to use the 'cash basis'. In this instance, income received and expenses paid in the year can be taken into account.

For UK residents, self-assessment means that a separate schedule should be requested with the tax return headed 'Land and Property'. Tax will be due on the rental income on 31 January and 31 July each year, assuming overall liability is above certain minimum limits.

What is a legitimate expense?

Always be aware that expenses must be incurred 'wholly and exclusively' for business purposes and must not be of a capital nature. To avoid any dispute, retain full records to substantiate that expenses are deductible.

Determining whether something is a capital expense or an income expense is not always easy and the line drawn between the two is sometimes difficult to determine. If, for example, roof tiles are replaced following a storm, this would be considered to be a repair. If, however, it was considered that a significant improvement had been made to the roof beyond its original condition, then that would be a capital expenditure. Common examples of repairs that are normally deductible as income expenses are exterior and interior painting and decorating, and mending broken windows, doors and furniture. However, care still needs to be taken as replacing single-glazed with double-glazed units is clearly a capital improvement, but replacing single-glazed units with new and equivalent single-glazed units is a deductible expense.

A good illustration of the 'wholly and exclusively' rule is in connection with travelling. The cost of travel between different properties solely for the purpose of dealing with rental business is deductible, but travel costs from your home to the letting property and back will only be allowable if the visit is exclusively business related. In other words, if you stop off during the journey for some other purpose, this would not meet the 'wholly and exclusively' rule. As indicated earlier, a clear understanding of the rules and regulations is essential in maximising the amount of allowable expenses generally.

Joint or sole name ownership?

It is vital to consider at the outset the ownership basis of the property. If, for example, ownership was held jointly by a husband and wife, then one half of any profit would be the husband's and one half the wife's. If the husband works while his wife is based at home looking after the children (or vice versa), then the husband's half-share may well be taxable at the highest rate of 40 per cent. But, if the property was in the wife's sole name, this could mean that the profit would be partially covered by her tax free personal allowance and then only chargeable at 20 per cent on the first £4,100 and 23 per cent on profit over £4,100 and under £26,100, as Example 10 illustrates (see pages 142–143).

(continues on page 144)

EXAMPLE 10

A comparison of the tax payable on a jointly owned property and a property solely in the wife's name

- If the property is jointly owned, the couple's total tax bill is £10,794 (£9,547 for the husband plus £1,247 for the wife).
- If the property is bought solely in the wife's name, the couple's total tax bill is £9,119 (£5,572 for the husband plus £3,547 for the wife).
- The tax saved when the property is put in the wife's name is £1,675.

JOINTLY OWNED PROPERTY

Net rental income = £20,000

Tax comparison

	Husband		Wife
	£		£
Salary	30,000		–
Rent (half-share each)	10,000		10,000
Total gross income	**£40,000**		**£10,000**
Personal tax allowance (1997/98)	4,045		4,045
Taxable income	**£35,955**		**£5,955**
Tax payable:			
4,100 @ 20%	820	4,100 @ 20%	820
22,000 @ 23%	5,060	1,855 @ 23%	427
9,855 @ 40%	3,942		
Total tax payable	**£9,822**		**£1,247**
Less the married couples' allowance:			
1,830 @ 15%	275		–
Total tax due	**£9,547**		**£1,247**

PROPERTY IN WIFE'S SOLE NAME

Net rental income = £20,000

Tax comparison

	Husband	Wife
	£	£
Salary	30,000	–
Rent (half-share)	–	20,000
Total gross income	**£30,000**	**£20,000**
Personal tax allowance (1997/98)	4,045	4,045
Taxable income	**£25,955**	**£15,955**

Tax payable:

4,100 @ 20%		820	4,100 @ 20%	820
21,855 @ 23%		5,027	11,855 @ 23%	2,727
Total tax payable		**£5,847**		**£3,547**

Less the married couples' allowance:

1,830 @ 15%	275	–

Total tax due	**£5,572**	**£3,547**

The interest element

One of the big advantages of an investment property is that all interest, whatever the size of the loan, is fully deductible for tax purposes. It is very significant that the relief is not restricted to the normal £30,000 as it is under the MIRAS scheme and that such relief is effectively given at the individual's top rate of tax rather than limited to 10 per cent as it is under MIRAS.

However, it is important to be aware that the allowance of all interest against tax applies only if the loan is taken out to purchase or improve a property and that such a loan is taken out at the time of purchase or quite shortly afterwards. Although the Inland Revenue does not always pick this up, if a property is bought for cash and a loan is taken out later, then it can successfully argue that the loan was not taken out for the purpose of buying or improving the property and therefore that no interest is allowable against tax.

Capital gains tax

The amount of capital gains tax (CGT) payable on even a substantial profit is often not as large as many people imagine because of indexation relief. This takes into account the effects of inflation and can quite dramatically reduce the profit for tax purposes. From March 1982, the effective start date for CGT purposes, indexation relief is worth in excess of 90 per cent of the original value. In other words, if a property cost £100,000 in March 1982, its value for CGT purposes in 1998 would be over £190,000. And, in addition to indexation relief, both husbands and wives have an annual exemption, which is currently £6,500 each.

It is worth remembering that CGT is charged at an individual's highest income tax rate, which may be another good reason for considering purchasing a property in the wife's sole name.

Inheritance tax

Inheritance tax is largely governed by a person's domicile status. Domicile is a legal status and is a concept that is distinct from a person's residential status. The question of domicile can often involve complex negotiations with the UK tax authorities and professional advice is usually necessary. Basically, your domicile is your homeland, so for those who are born in and remain in the United Kingdom you are almost certainly domiciled here. UK domiciled individuals are liable to inheritance tax in respect of their worldwide assets. Non-domiciled individuals are usually only liable to inheritance tax on assets situated in the UK and have various tax planning opportunities available to them. One of these would be to investigate the ownership of property through an offshore company or trust. Although this is a complex area, it can provide significant advantages. Once again, professional advice is essential if you decide to pursue this route.

Furnished holiday lettings

As indicated at the beginning of the chapter, there are specific rules and regulations relating to holiday letting, but they do provide important opportunities, particularly for UK residents. Losses can be offset against other income, the income itself is classified as earnings and therefore retirement annuity and personal pension plan contributions can be considered for tax-saving purposes, capital allowances can be obtained on furniture and furnishings, and CGT 'roll-over' and retirement relief can be claimed.

To be regarded as holiday accommodation, a property must be available for commercial letting to the public as holiday accommodation for at least 140 days in a 12-month period, and be let for at least 70 such days. Under normal circumstances, it must not be under the same occupation for more than 31 consecutive days at any time during a period of 7 months in that 12-month period.

If the individual has more than one property available for holiday letting, it is not necessary for each property to be actually let for 70 days provided that each one satisfies the 140 day and 7 month rules. You may, in fact, take an average over all relevant properties to satisfy the 70 day rule.

Landlords not resident in the UK

An individual who does not reside in the United Kingdom has no immunity from UK tax on rental income. In particular, it is important for expatriates to appreciate that the Taxes Act obliges all letting and managing agents to deduct tax from any rental income paid after certain expenses have been deducted. The agent will then account for this tax to the Inland Revenue on a quarterly basis and furthermore will submit annual returns providing the information about the expatriate and the property, the gross rent and the tax deducted. The agent will then in turn provide the expatriate with a tax certificate for use when preparing his own tax return. Where this is no agent involved, the same obligations will normally be passed to the tenant. However, there are limitations on a tenant's responsibilities – for example, if the rent is below £100 per week.

To avoid this situation, the expatriate investor can elect for the self-assessment system, which will enable the Inland Revenue to issue a tax approval certificate to the agent (or tenant), thus avoiding the deduction of tax at source. This brings with it certain responsibilities that have to be maintained, otherwise the certificate will be withdrawn and deductions commenced/recommenced. The investor has the responsibility to ensure that all tax matters are up to date, that he has a 'good tax history' (ie he must be seen to have paid past liabilities promptly and to have complied with the requirements of self-assessment including the filing of tax returns and payment of tax liabilities on time). It is quite clear that rather than simplifying matters, self-assessment has in many ways made compliance with the tax regulations more complex and care needs to be taken. This is particularly the case when the expatriate is confronted, not only with declaring his rental income, but also determining his residence status.

Crown servants

Crown servants working abroad find themselves in a less fortunate position than their commercial counterpart in that their salaries remain liable for tax in the United Kingdom. Therefore, if rental income is received, this will be added to the salary and taxed at the highest appropriate rate. For crown servants, the simple tax planning opportunity illustrated in Example 10 (see pages 142–143) might prove useful.

Capital gains tax

Individuals not resident in the United Kingdom will be exempt from CGT and if they have been abroad for more than 36 months, they can sell an asset without being liable to CGT right up to the time of their return. Those who have been abroad for less than this period of time must dispose of any asset before the end of the tax year preceding their arrival if they wish to avoid CGT.

This obviously provides for planning opportunities, as profits can be taken free of UK liability. However, care is required as regards liability in the country you are leaving. If, unfortunately, a capital loss has been made, then the property should be sold after return to the United Kingdom so that it may be utilised against future gains.

Beware over-trading

Whether the investor is resident overseas or in the United Kingdom, he should be aware that if he buys and sells property too frequently there is a risk that the Inland Revenue will treat him as carrying on a trade rather than realising capital gains. The impact of this is particularly severe in the case of an investor resident overseas who would otherwise pay no tax at all on capital gains.

Therefore, if an investor has bought and sold a number of investment properties in the space of 12 months, the Inland Revenue could argue that the investor is carrying on the trade of dealing in properties, and the gains would be subject to income tax rather than being assessed for CGT. If an overseas resident is frequently trading in properties, it may well make sense to consider buying through other members of his family or through individual limited companies.

SUMMARY

◆ It is advisable to approach a specialist tax firm before committing to purchase any property investment whether you are a non-resident of the United Kingdom or a non-domiciliary.

◆ Ownership of investment property, even if it is just one property, is now treated as a business by the Inland Revenue with all the tax advantages that that brings.

◆ One of the big advantages of an investment property is that all interest, whatever the size of the loan, is, in most circumstances, fully deductible for tax purposes.

EPILOGUE

Reading this book will, I hope, help you to avoid the mistakes that I made in my early years and so quickly become a successful property investor. This book has been written to enable readers to maximise profits from investing in residential property to let and by carefully following its guidelines, I have no doubt it will be successful in this regard.

By definition, buying a property for investment means that, in most circumstances, you will be the owner of two houses. However, there are many people with no home at all and so, having maximised gains for yourself, I would like you to consider supporting, in however small a way, an outstanding charity for the homeless called Emmaus. Twenty-five per cent of the profits from this book are being donated to Emmaus and I hope that you may, when you know a little bit more about Emmaus, wish to contribute a small percentage of your personal gains from investing in property. Emmaus is a special charity because its aim is to help homeless people help themselves and not simply to provide a roof over their heads. The Right Reverend Lord Runcie is President of Emmaus UK and in a recent review of the achievements of the charity, he commented as follows.

'There is no doubt that this is the most exciting and successful development that I have known in long experience of projects for the homeless. It deals with single, homeless, unemployed people and it brings them into sensible, self-supporting communities. It really does work. I have watched it from its beginnings in Cambridge and we now have embryo communities all over the country.'

Terry Waite CBE is the Chairman of the Appeal Committee for Emmaus. The following is an extract from a letter dated 24 September 1997 to me.

'I enclose a copy of the Appeal brochure. As someone who has spent five years in captivity – an extreme form of homelessness – I know what this project can achieve. May I urge you to support this remarkable self-help scheme. As you will have noted, we are only appealing for funds to provide a home and a job for those in need. Beyond that (and I want to emphasise this), for its continued existence, the Community is totally self-supporting.'

For further details, please contact: The Emmaus Appeal Office, PO Box 854, Landbeach, Cambridge CB4 4GR, UK (Tel/Fax: 01223 862676; E-mail: emmaus-cam@dial.pipex.com).

Malcolm Walton
February 1998

USEFUL ADDRESSES

Buying agents specialising in investment property

London

The County Homesearch Company Ltd
1A, 18 The Coda Centre
189 Munster Road
London SW6 6AW
Tel: 0171 386 7222
Fax: 0171 386 7444

Greene & Greene
27 Montpelier Street
Knightsbridge
London SW7 1HF
Tel: 0171 225 1616
Fax: 0171 581 0189

Japan Property Investment Service
2 Queens Drive
West Acton
Ealing
London W3 0HA
Tel: 0181 752 0445
Fax: 0181 752 0219

Perry Bousfield International
36 Bruton Street
Mayfair
London W1X 7DD
Tel: 0171 409 2131
Fax: 0171 629 1262

Property Vision
8 Cromwell Place
London SW7 2JN
Tel: 0171 823 8388
Fax: 0171 823 8188

Quality Street Ltd
108–110 Finchley Road
London NW3 5JJ
Tel: 0171 431 3700
Fax: 0171 431 6166

Senate International (London) Ltd
15 Hanover Square
London W1R 9AJ
Tel: 0171 408 2444
Fax: 0171 493 4319

Bath & Bristol

The County Homesearch Company Ltd
25 Manilla Road
Clifton
Bristol BS8 4EB
Tel: 0117 974 1569
Fax: 0117 973 2050

Expatriate Property Services
28 Queens Square
Bristol BS1 14ND
Tel: 0117 925 0967
Fax: 0117 925 0970

Cambridge

Senate International
8 Kings Parade
Cambridge CB2 1SJ
Tel: 01223 300012
Fax: 01223 300013

Spires International
185 East Road
Cambridge CB1 1BG
Tel: 01223 300903
Fax: 01223 358903

Edinburgh

Albany Property Services
113 Piersfield Terrace
Edinburgh EH8 7BS
Tel: 0131 652 0445
Fax: 0131 652 0445

Crichton-Stuart Associates
20 Manor Place
Edinburgh EH3 7DS
Tel: 0131 220 4817
Fax: 0131 226 2135

Bruce Rae Property Management
132 St Stephen Street
Edinburgh EH3 5AA
Tel: 0131 220 0303
Fax: 0131 220 0440

Senate International
20 Charlotte Square
Edinburgh EH2 4DF
Tel: 0131 226 3638
Fax: 0131 226 3639

Glasgow

Quality Street Ltd
130 St Vincent Street
Glasgow G2 5HF
Tel: 0141 248 4553
Fax: 0141 204 0573

Senate International
c/o 20 Charlotte Square
Edinburgh EH2 4DF
Tel: 0131 226 3638
Fax: 0131 226 3639

Nottingham

Senate International
149 Derby Road
Nottingham NG7 1ND
Tel: 0115 988 1933
Fax: 0115 988 1944

Oxford

Finders Keepers
1 Vineyard Chambers
Abingdon
Oxon OX14 3PX
Tel: 01235 535454
Fax: 01235 535575

**The County Homesearch
Company Ltd**
Dormer House
Somerton
Oxford OX6 4LP
Tel: 01869 345736
Fax: 01869 345738

Senate International
29 Beaumont Street
Oxford OX2 2NU
Tel: 01865 556002
Fax: 01865 556065

Sheffield

**The County Homesearch
Company Ltd**
6 Betcheman Gardens
Sheffield S10 3FW
Tel: 0114 268 2533
Fax: 0114 267 9265

Letting & management agents with property investment buying arms

London

**Featherstones
(I D & M) Co Ltd**
17 Trinity Road
London SW17 7SD
Tel: 0181 767 1234
Fax: 0181 682 1312

Foxtons Property Search
92 Park Lane
London W1Y 4EJ
Tel: 0171 973 2995
Fax: 0171 973 2001

London (continued)

London Home Rentals
27 Thurloe Street
South Kensington
London SW7 2LQ
Tel: 0171 838 1111
Fax: 0171 589 1188

Ludlow Thompson
3–5 Dock Street
London E1 8JN
Tel: 0171 480 6815
Fax: 0171 480 7717

Savills
1 Barclay Street
London W1X 5AA
Tel: 0171 499 8644
Fax: 0171 495 3773

Bath

Black Horse Agencies
Alder King
4 Princes Buildings
George Street
Bath BA1 2ED
Tel: 01225 469882
Fax: 01225 445207

Cluttons
23 Gay Street
Bath BA1 2NS
Tel: 01225 447575
Fax: 01225 446089

Bristol

Allen & Harris
436–440 Gloucester Road
Horfield
Bristol BS7 8TX
Tel: 0117 924 1999
Fax: 0117 923 2274

Black Horse Agencies
Alder King
94E Whiteladies Road
Clifton
Bristol BS8 2XR
Tel: 0117 973 8915
Fax: 0117 923 7980

Cambridge

Bidwells
Trumpington Road
Cambridge CB2 2LD
Tel: 01223 841842
Fax: 01223 840721

Camflats
Elmhurst
22a Brooklands Avenue
Cambridge CB2 2DQ
Tel: 01223 350800
Fax: 01223 353729

Cambridge (continued)

Savills
24 Hills Road
Cambridge CB2 1JW
Tel: 01223 322955
Fax: 01223 322493

Edinburgh

D J Alexander
52–54 Dundas Street
Edinburgh EH3 6QZ
Tel: 0131 558 3000
Fax: 0131 558 3005

Braemore
Brae House, 53 Dundas St
Edinburgh EH3 6RS
Tel: 0131 624 6666
Fax: 0131 624 6664

Glasgow

Alan & Harris
115 Byres Road
Glasgow G11 5HW
Tel: 0141 339 3103
Fax: 0141 339 7655

Fine Homes Letting Agency
75 St Vincent Street
Glasgow G2 5UB
Tel: 0141 221 7993
Fax: 0141 204 4164

Countrywide Residential Letting
153 Buchanan Street
Glasgow G1 2JX
Tel: 0141 221 7211
Fax: 0141 221 7103

Nottingham

Countrywide Property Management
65/66 Long Row
Nottingham NG1 6JN
Tel: 0115 958 3887
Fax: 0115 958 3891

Savills
4 St Peters Gate
Nottingham NG2 1JG
Tel: 0115 958 6161
Fax: 0115 955 2103/04

Nottingham (continued)

Spencer Birch
10 Kings Walk
Trinity Square
Nottingham NG1 2AE
Tel: 0115 941 3678
Fax: 0115 950 6235

Oxford

Adkins
12/13 St Clements
Oxford OX4 1YG
Tel: 01865 764533
Fax: 01865 764777

Chancellors
107 London Road
Headington
Oxford OX3 9HZ
Tel: 01865 763464
Fax: 01865 741146

Mortgage brokers specialising in sourcing mortgage deals for buying investment property

Chase De Vere
Ryder Court
14 Ryder Street
St James's
London SW1Y 6QB
Tel: 0171 930 7242
Fax: 0171 930 3691

John Charcoal
10–12 Great Queen Street
Holborn
London WC2B 5DD
Tel: 0171 611 7000
Fax: 0171 611 7010

**International
Mortgage Plans**
11 Woodview Court
Queens Road
Weybridge
Surrey KT1 9XF
Tel: 01932 830660
Fax: 01932 829603

Contract furnishers

Edwin Clark
The Contracts Furniture
Specialists
  The Carrington Building
  1–5 Colonial Drive
  Bollo Lane
  Chiswick
  London W4 5NU
  Tel: 0181 932 6292
  Fax: 0181 932 6299

Elite Furniture Contracts
  121 Moffat Street
  Glasgow G5 ONG
  Tel: 0141 429 1124
  Fax: 0141 429 1599

Forrest Furnishing
  1174 South Street
  Glasgow G14 0AL
  Fax: 0141 300 7460
  Tel: 0141 300 7400

Denis Green & Partners
  Home Furnishings
  8–10 Market Square
  Witney
  Oxon OX8 7BB
  Tel: 01993 703450
  Fax: 01993 703513

M A S Furniture
Contracts Ltd
  M A S House
  374–378 Old Street
  London EC1V 9LT
  Tel: 0171 739 6961
  Fax: 0171 739 2256

Orchid Interiors
  66 Banfield House
  London SW6 3SJ
  Tel: 0171 602 0055
  Fax: 0171 371 3113

Specialist tax advisers

W T Fry
  Crescent House
  Crescent Road
  Worthing
  West Sussex BN11 1RN
  Tel: 01903 231545
  Fax: 01903 200868

Peters, Elworthy & Moore
  Salisbury House
  Station Road
  Cambridge CB1 2LA
  Tel: 01223 362333
  Fax: 01223 461424

Lakin Rose
  Enterprise House
  Vision Park
  Histon
  Cambridge CB4 4ZR
  Tel: 01223 235707
  Fax: 01223 235808

General

Association of Residential Letting Agents (Arla)
Maple House
53–55 Woodside Road
Amersham
Bucks HP6 6AA
Hotline: 01923 896555
Tel: 01494 431680
Fax: 01494 431530

Association of Relocation Agents (ARA)
Premier House
11 Marlborough Place
Brighton BN1 1UB
Tel: 01273 683604
Fax: 01273 624455
Provides details of all
main relocation agents
operating in the UK

The Consumer Safety Unit
Department of Trade and
Industry
Room 302
10–18 Victoria Street
London SW1H 0NN
Tel: 0171 510 0151

Estates Gazette Auction Fax Line
5–7 Old Town
Clapham
London SW4 0JT
Tel: 0171 720 5000
Fax: 0171 720 5050

Halifax Quarterley Review
Halifax plc
Trinity Road, Halifax
West Yorkshire HX1 2RG
Tel: 01422 333333
Fax: 01422 332043

Independent Housing Ombudsman
Mr Roger Jeffries
Norman House
105–109 The Strand
London WC2R 0AA
Tel: 0171 836 3630

Let Sure Credit Search
Premier House
Bradford Road
Cleckheaton
West Yorkshire BD19 3TT
Tel: 0345 697543
Fax: 0345 697544

National Land Finding Agency
Rood End House
6 Stortford Road
Great Dunmow
Essex CM6 1DA
Tel: 01371 876875
Fax: 01279 656999

Pavillion FCC Credit Referencing
1 The Briars
Waterbury Drive
Waterlooville
Hampshire PO7 7YH
Tel: 01705 232235
Fax: 01705 232126

Joseph Rowntree Foundation
The University of York
Centre for Housing Policy
Heslington
York YO1 5DD
Tel: 01904 433691
Fax: 01904 432318

The Small Landlords Association
53 Werter Road
London SW15 2LL
Tel: 0181 780 9954

FURTHER READING

Building Your Own Home
by Murray Armor
The Book Service Ltd
Colchester Road
Frating Green
Colchester
Essex CO7 7DW
Tel: 01206 213577

Furniture & Fire Safety
The Consumer Safety Unit
Department of Trade and Industry
Room 302
10–18 Victoria Street
London SW1H 0NN
Tel: 0171 510 0151

Investing in Residential Property
A practical 'how to' guide to long and holiday lettings
by David and Hilary Humphries
UNiSkiLL Ltd
Eynsham
Oxon OX8 1TH
Tel: 01865 883655

Self Build Magazine
Waterways World Ltd
The Well House
High Street
Burton-on-Trent
Staffs DE14 1JQ
Tel: 01283 742950

The Which Guide to Renting and Letting
Which? Ltd
2 Marylebone Road
London NW1 4DF
Tel: 0171 830 6000

INDEX